Ethics and the War on Terrorism

Kenneth L. Vaux
Professor of Theological Ethics
Garrett Evangelical Theological Seminary

WIPF and Stock Publishers
EUGENE, OREGON

Wipf and Stock Publishers
150 West Broadway
Eugene OR 97401

Ethics and the War on Terrorism
By Kenneth L. Vaux
ISBN: 1-57910-941-1

Printed May 2002

Contents

Acknowledgements

I thank Andy Watts for his assistance and my son Bert for stimulating discussion and for editing the manuscript. To my colleagues at Garrett Seminary and First Presbyterian Church, Evanston, I am indebted for refining the convictions of this essay. I dedicate it to three pioneers of justice in the anguish of this hour: Drs. David Handley, Don Wagner, and Peter Knobel.

1

Introduction

"Other evils there are that may come...yet it is not our part to master all the tides of the world, but to do what is in us for the succor of those years wherein we are set."

Gandalf the Wizard
The Lord of the Rings, Book V, Chapter 9

Composed initially in the ominous years of the 1930's when war clouds hovered over the world, J. R. R. Tolkien sent the first draft to his son, an RAF pilot in North Africa. The Lord of the Rings was high-level mythology seeking to explain immediate crisis within ultimate truth and inspire people through the concrete historic good and evil then and ever unfolding in the world. As the so-called "Operation Enduring Freedom" – the war in Afghanistan – wanes and the eerie dust cloud subsides in ground zero of Manhattan, thoughtful people around the world seem bewildered.

They agree with moderate Muslim voices that the U.S. has provoked a fanatic hatred, even suicidal rage, by its propping up of tyrannical Arabian governments, its uncritical underwriting of Israel's oppression and occupation of the Palestinians and the lingering infanticidal sanctions and "saber rattling" against the people of Iraq. But they also concur with Israel that:

- the atrocity visited by Christendom on Jewry for a millennium — crusades, pogroms, ghettos and holocaust — necessitated actualizing the ancient dream of a Holy land nation, to found the state of Israel;
- in a terrifying world weapons of mass destruction must not fall into irresponsible hands;
- the persistent suicidal violence of Hamas and Islamic Jihad must cease if the State of Israel is to be secured, and the moral soul of the world be saved.

The way through this bewildering ambivalence takes us up against the trifurcated story of the faith peoples of Abraham: Judaism, Christianity and Islam. The holy passions of these three movements—the communities of Hagar, Sarah and Rachel; of Abraham, Isaac and Ishmael—somehow simmer the tensions and sustain the creativities of the secular histories which they underlie. To borrow from Abraham Lincoln, "We all knew that somehow [Israel] was a cause of that war."

Now, at the turn of the twenty-first century, in the lands of the Afghans and of other Muslims on the rim of Orthodox-Christic—recently communistic Russia; in old Persia—Iran and Iraq; in Indonesia; in Palestine/Israel and adjacent Arabic lands; in Africa where Christianity and Islam interplay with resurgent indigenous faiths; even in Europe and the U.S., as cells in New Jersey, Florida, Detroit—this drama—a holy passion play—is being enacted, and we struggle to apprehend its meaning.

This monograph seeks to further that inquiry. It is a formulation providing the groundwork for my seminary class "War and Peace", and an adult class at my home congregation—First Presbyterian, Evanston. It explains my persuasion that the root cause of the war on terrorism, declared by President George Bush, Jr. on September 11, 2001, is an historical-faith crisis whose epicenter is Israel. But lest we rise too quickly in condemnation, we must remember that the agony of Israel also involves a prior humiliation imposed on Palestine and Islam by machinations of the West in the disintegration of the Ottoman Empire. The present crisis is also related to that most-profound evil, the grievous Holocaust and complicity in Holocaust against Jewish people by Christian Europe and America at mid-century. To the forgiveness of that same Christian world she has stood with Muslims in Bosnia and Kosovo and has gone to the death to defeat Hitler's genocidal anti-Semitism, Mussolini and Japan's fascism as well as Russian and Asian communism. Yet accountability for the war on terrorism reaches out into all three Abrahamic religions. Andrew Sullivan may be right when he suggests that "...something inherent in religious monotheism...lends itself to terrorist temptation." ("This is a Religious War," *New York Times Magazine*, October 7, 2001, p. 47.)

In all this therefore I will search out the religious (spiritual and moral) passion which animates war history and the war on terrorism. I will appreciatively assess the justice and irenic elements of that passion while condemning as faithless its idolatry and violence.

While sharing Andrew Sullivan's horror at faith-induced violence, I contend that this malign action has come from politically co-opted religion not from the genuine faith and morality which is born and sustained in monotheistic, Decalogic and akedic theology. (By *akedah* I am referring to the central belief in commandment, sacrifice, death and resurrection conveyed through the three faiths in the Abraham/Isaac [Messianic] event.)

In the biblical tradition streaming from Abraham this composite conviction is called wisdom.

The argument will proceed as follows: On the questions of faith-substance I will seek to clearly show what is authentic and antithetic to the particular faith/morality traditions in this war history. Declension from true faith prompts impiety which inevitably creates injustice—and war. Historically I will traverse back and forth from the contemporary war on terrorism to Holy War in biblical Israel; from the modern wars against fascism and communism to primitive Christian pacifism, and Constantinian Empire establishment; from the religious and Cousins' wars—so constitutive of our modern crises of secularity and power to the fatal antagonistic trifurcation of Abrahamic faith in the period from the rise of Islam, through the Crusades and beyond. Finally, we will evaluate the present situation. This sequential survey after a statement of the hypothesis to be tested in this study.

Thesis

War is half-right. We are obliged to defend and extend the good. We are compelled to broadcast faith and exemplify ethic. Spiritual and intellectual passion, expressed in what we call proselytism, evangelization and Jihad, among Abraham's three children, is legitimate and honorable. On occasion even the use of force is justified. Such peace/war has therefore been rationalized in the theories of "holy" and "just" war. Wars to resist tyranny, protect freedom, effect justice and establish peace, even with occasional resort to arms, are morally obligatory. Hitler and Osama bin Laden so concentrate evil, inhumanity and godlessness that bringing such culprits to justice—human and divine, even capital sentence, is justified. Peace making and peacekeeping requires resistance to evil.

But there is the other half. War is seldom right and good. It most often serves sub-ultimate goals of land grabbing, power assertion and economic expediency. The long arc of history most often shows conflict arising from misunderstandings, lies, grievances—provoking overreactions, and foolhardy pride. All religion, ethics, philosophy, law and politics reject this folly and pretension. Surrealistic star wars with no casualties such as we have witnessed in Kuwait and now Afghanistan, obscure the harsh reality that all-out war in our age of capacity for mass destruction (nuclear, biological, chemical) is suicidal.

Just War theory resonates this value contending that the only legitimate reason for war is to restore peace by instituting justice. This notion is as old as Hebraic and Hellenic Holy War. That there can be no peace without justice is the central contention of the broad Abrahamic tradition. Shalom is a state of well-being. Biblical peace is not merely the absence of war. A state of affairs that can be called righteousness entails respect and provision for the poor and oppressed, true freedom, domestic and global imputing of dignity to all persons and a deep love of peace!

Our thesis therefore holds that spiritual intensity in service of the God of Israel—of Abraham, Isaac and Jacob—requires contention to do justice, love, mercy (forgiveness) and walk humbly with God (Torah) (Micah 6:8). War should only be decalogic or war "of the lamb." This essence of what we will describe as "rightful war" derived from "YAHWEH War" resonates with authentic Christian "crusade" and intellectual and prophetic "Jihad" in Islam. To seize the stark apocalyptic tongue of Bach's Christmas Hymn, *Break Forth O Beauteous Heavenly Light*, we seek that contention wherein "the power of Satan [is] breaking our peace eternal making."

But before we begin to explicate this distinction between legitimate and illegitimate war, holy and unholy passion, let us lay alongside our normative thesis a parallel empirical observation. Abrahamic holy passion passes through the layers of biblical and post biblical history in Israel, then into pacific, primitive, then militant Catholic Christianity, then into Islamic Jihad, specifically through responsive antagonism to aggressive Judaism and Christianity, then finally into Protestant-Puritan Christianity. This latest spiritual-moral mutation finally fashions an antagonism that William Cavanaugh will call the secular deification of the modern nation state, which is epitomized in Clauswitzian political war. Now the ultimate war—what we euphemistically call the Star Wars, but in actuality became the wars on terrorism—brings us to an age when true religious war must become a war against war. We must today wage a war of religion against the bellic war of state Machiavellian power disguised as religion. The co-optation of divine war by political entities is the ultimate blasphemy, idolatry and immorality.

The epitome of the crisis which engulfs the world today, what is called "The War on Terrorism" has to do with the establishment of the State of Israel in Palestine in the mid-twentieth century. This implantation was necessitated by that final violence of the Christian anti-Semitic crusade co-opted by the pagan, secular state—the Holocaust. Just as the Roman Empire's Shoah against ancient Israel is context for the Messiah's death, so his resurrection life is hope for the present Shoah. Here in the Third Reich, a demonic modern secular state joined ancient pagan elements of violence to Christian antipathies toward Jews to seek to exterminate Abraham's first people. That crisis had to do therefore with Constantine's settlement and Christian empire and the medieval crusades against Judaism and Islam and with the counter action of Islamic Jihad that was precipitated by that aggression.

In the early modern period as Judaism assimilates into Western culture under threat of pogrom and ghettoization and as Islam is reshaped by the Ottoman Empire and as it strained for relevance, Protestantism emerges in the long and most decisive spiritual and moral revolution in human history. This epoch stretching from Wyclif to Wesley in 14th to 18th century Britain and its American plantation, the Anglo-American revolution, has become the ultimate determinative force in modern history—a benign yet malign bestowal. So to this curse/blessing we must repair.

To paraphrase Kevin Phillips in his *The Cousins' Wars* (New York: Basic Books, 1999), to possess a linguistic and commercial hegemony in the world is to convey, even coerce, a world view and ethic—a theology and a way of life—on that world. A new world empire has been born. We, today's Anglo-Americans, must assume a responsibility for what that world is now become—its glories and its disgraces. The U.S., I believe, has aspired to and therefore has assumed global supremacy. We must now, in partnership with other nations, lead the world not only in an extirpation of evil (terrorism) but also in the achievement of social justice, the reduction of poverty and the development of economic prosperity and peace. President Bush's pledge at the development summit in Mexico to strengthen the US commitments to alleviate world poverty we know is the best weapon against terrorism.

Put another way, if Max Weber's thesis is correct, then Protestant-Puritanism, the theology and lifestyle of Anglo-America with its precursors and counterparts on the European continent, fashions not only the age of liberalism and enterprise but also the age of power and usurpation. This religion not only liberates, it subjugates. It has its way in yet antagonizes the world. This public theology is one of the ultimate causes of what the world has become. To impose one's nation and ideology, one's *Weltanschauung* or religion on the world provokes the ire of even tolerant Islam. I contend that the war of terrorism can only be fathomed within this frame of reference.

When on September 11, 2001 Al Qaeda targets the World Trade Center and the Pentagon, they attack derivative manifestations of a belief system and a way of life. This way of life, "The American Way," according to Weberians, intensifies into the belief-action yield of world history (the Protestant Reformation). Capitalism, military power in the safeguard of freedom, constitutional democracy and human-rights-grounded social policy, are symbols of that particular "Holy passion." Each of these active values has creative and destructive manifestation. Economic free enterprise, now couched in "global economy," enhances opportunity for entrepreneurial persons. It also increases inequality and the polarity of rich and poor. Adam Smith and Karl Marx saw clearly the two sides of this Janus-faced coin.

Without social and distributive justice there can be no true entrepreneurial freedom. Free enterprise in its broad cultural impact, in other words, liberates and oppresses. Cooperation enlivens, competition emasculates. Capitalism converts and angers. South Korea capitulates, North Korea balks. This dimension of spirit, to use a concept employed by Hegel and Tillich, is in part behind military events like the Russian revolution, the Cuban missile crisis and the battle for Kandahar.

I argue that concrete cultural ideas and practices are ultimately theologically grounded:

> a concept of freedom rises from
> a vision of man which arises from
> a soteriology (i.e., a view of ultimate efficacy) which arises from
> a view of God.

Though Kevin Phillips remains a descriptive historian and hesitates to offer a normative thesis, I find corroboration of my thesis in his work. I will argue that "The Cousins' Wars" – the Anglican-Puritan campaign which has changed modern history—is ethical when it is a "YAWEH war," a "war of the Lamb" – a war for justice, righteousness and peace. When it becomes war for some sub-ultimate good – war for the "American way" or "American Power" it becomes idolatrous and immoral.

Jared Diamond's *Guns, Germs and Steel* (Norton: London, 1997) is a search for "ultimate explanations" for patterns of human history especially the life patterns of peoples on continents. The anthropologist gives signature to his study by "posing" Yali's question, which he heard from a native of Papua, New Guinea:

> Why is it that you white people developed so much <u>cargo</u> (steel, axes, matches, medicines, clothing, soft drinks, umbrellas, cigarettes)..." and brought it to New Guinea, but we black people had so little <u>cargo</u> of our own? (57).

Diamond contends that the peoples of Eurasia and their transplants to North America seek to dominate the world with wealth and power. The deleterious progression from concept and conviction to coercion goes like this:

God creates freedom
⇓

freedom stimulates entrepreneurial enterprise
⇓

enterprise seeks to exploit peoples and markets
⇓

thereby establishing domination.

A Darwinian view

The theological and moral inferences and insinuations of this sequencing are mine. Diamond seeks merely to describe a cultural phenomenon. In quasi-Weberian terms he ponders the empirical fact that some peoples seek to consolidate wealth and power and rise in dominance while others live with more contentment and passivity. In the war thesis that I offer, confrontation and engagement, including the initial response of defensive security, are born either in prideful and aggressive malice or in a worthy search to "deliver from evil." Diamond's premise of biological determinism obscures the fundamental reality of moral freedom and responsibility.

Another erudite historian-philosopher of war is Victor Davis Hanson. In his *The Soul of Battle* (New York: Anchor, 1999) and *Carnage and Culture* (New York: Doubleday, 2001), he roots the inclination toward war in the very encouragement and exhilaration of freedom. From the earliest battles of the Greeks against the Persians in 480 BC near Salamis, through the Tet offensive in Viet Nam, the impulse of a democratic vision of liberty itself prompted not only vigorous securing protectiveness of that "way of life" but a forceful preemptive, even aggressive strike mentality to promulgate that value.

> Adherence to structures of constitutional government, capitalism, freedom of religious and political association, free speech and intellectual tolerance" produced a soldier who can "kill like none other on the planet. (*Carnage and Culture*, 17.)

This "Braveheart," "Duke (Wayne)," even "Ali" image of the primal, paradigmatic warrior as a cultural prototype runs deep in all human communities. Even that godly warrior, St. Michael against the dragon, Saint Sebastian, (or his Tolkien counterpart Boromir) against the arrows of evil, sanctifies this icon. But this is not the same as my theological premise.

Though the martyr image of St. Sebastian or the Jesuit priest cast crucified over the Ecuadorian falls in *The Mission* comes close to my concept, i.e. living for the name, the truth, the way, even at the cost of one's life ("to love God with all one's soul" - Mark 12:30), the concept of righteous war which I offer is first, war for God alone, second, war for right (truth, justice, peace), third, war which desists and disowns penultimate ambitions and pretensions. International terror, national and homeland security can become a theological idol, displacing *shalom*. The motto of Abraham Lincoln's political theology is not "my country (*Heimat*) right or wrong," but "with my country when right, against her when wrong."

The thesis that I offer therefore can be summarized in the following postulates:

- God (the deity discerned by Abraham) wills singular devotion, human freedom, human justice and peace (walking in the God-way).
- Humans and their various communities are called to defend and extend that faith and life.
- The mechanisms of news (gospel), the just society (*tikkun olam*) and Jihad (Islam) are the human concomitants of the divine real-building in the world.
- "Setting free the oppressed, good news to the poor, proclamation of Jubilee," (Luke 4:18).
- "Just" ("right") war is defending and extending that good on earth.

The stipulates of Just War: *jus ad bello* and *jus ad bellum* pertain:

- only attack justifies assault: perpetual peace
- broadest legitimate authority, e.g. UN.
- protect innocents (civilians)
- efforts must not involve violence or vengeance
- bring to justice and trial (no assassination)
- restoration of peace (with justice) is the ultimate end of war.

At this point, having introduced a normative theory about war-making, let us take up dialogue with several important twentieth century "good war," "just war "thinkers. Before we conclude the introduction to our argument we need to set out some corroborative ideas from several ethicists who have addressed the morality of war in general. Two secular Jews and two evangelical-Protestant Christians present an interesting variety of views all within the parameters of the norm I am proposing. Studs Terkel (*The Good War*), Michael Walzer (*Just and Unjust Wars*), Paul Ramsey (*War and the Christian Conscience*, *Just War*) and John Howard Yoder (*The Politics of Jesus*) offer nuance and critique, sharpening and offering definition to our proposed "rule of war."

Resonant voices

Studs Terkel
Chicago's laureate narrator has chronicled through many voices *The Good War* (New York: The New Press, 1984). This phrase, prefaces Terkel, "has been frequently voiced by men of his (interviewees) and my generation, to distinguish that war from other wars, declared and undeclared" (p. vi.) Interviews with Marcel Ophels and Arno Mayer, Telford Taylor, Ken Galbraith and others touch on the Holocaust which was the root evil of Nazism (and, I contend, the wars against communism and terrorism). To turn vice President Cheney's misplaced recent rhetoric in the Middle East,

here "civilization" was really "at stake." This oppression and genocide portended a loss of freedom for Europe, America and the world. This abstract rationale was little understood, and scarcely accessible to the conscience of the American and Russian, French and British soldiers who gave their lives to defeat Hitler. Yet the long twilight of Auschwitz and Buchenwald, the ovens and the ashes, would presage the dawn and phoenix awakening of humanity which would overtone, undergird and supply the intuitions and courage and become the significance of that "Great War."

Michael Walzer
Michael Walzer dedicates his masterful study of *Just and Unjust Wars* (New York: Basic Books, 1977) with the inscription on the Holocaust Memorial Yad Va-shem in Jerusalem.

> Aux martyrs de l'Holocauste
> Aux révoltés des Ghettos
> Aux partisans de forêts
> Aux insurgés des camps
> Aux combatants de la résistance
> Aux soldats des forces alliées
> Aux sauveteurs de fréres en peril
> Aux vaillants de l'imigration clandestine
> A l'éternite

Chastened by the moral ambiguity of the Vietnam War and instructed by his incisive studies of the Puritans, Walzer searches for a theologically sensitive political philosophy, one which probes for the consciousness of Exodus liberation and for the derivative passion for faith and righteousness which shapes the subsequent historical sagas of Israel/Judea. In his imagery (and mine) he searches for the root and character of the Abrahamic *Hegira* which interprets spiritual and political reality from Abraham's *akedah* to the Hebrew Exodus and Passover, through the concourse of Christianity in the Hellenic world and Roman Empire down to the Puritan revolution, the "Cousins' Wars," Viet Nam and beyond. Concretely he searches for secularly applicable philosophical-political guidelines for "going to" and "carrying on" war.

After establishing that war is an ethical quandary and conundrum and that human communities are by nature aggressive, Walzer expounds the War Convention. With compelling illustrations from actual war episodes, he shows the ethical strengths and ambiguities of the tradition we call "Just War."

Walzer's thesis corroborates that which I offer from the Akedic theology of Abrahamic faith. It finds the liberation from bondage (both external oppression and it's own violent prosperity experienced by biblical Israel) morally decisive and normatively instructive. This gift to humanity is accomplished, as freedom becomes faith-yielding justice through suffering and sacrifice. (Abraham's *hegira* and *akedah*).

The human doctrines at issue in war pertain to themes such as distributive justice, political duty or punishment—the domain of politics, philosophy and theology (sanctions, good and evil). Even governmental policy has often chosen to address issues of rectitude, "the divine will" and "good and evil" in a search for justification of action. This armchair philosophizing, which arises historically in post war hindsight, seems, at turn of the 21st century, to require wars where there can be no loss of life. They neglect the dirty, "war is hell," brutality of conflict. The incursion into Panama in 1989 was called "Operation Just Cause" (which Walzer adds, "it wasn't") and the response to Al Qaeda called "Operation Enduring Freedom" (2001). All such designation is suspect. Walzer notes the "perverse if exhilarating effects...whenever the language of holiness is taken over by politicians. ...politics and war are never holy—not, at least, as I understand holiness" (xi).

While I too object to using religious rhetoric to justify political ambition, with Andrew Sullivan I have been struck by the "general reluctance to call the conflict which began on September 11, a religious war" ("This Is a Religious War," *New York Times Magazine*, October 7, 2001, p. 44.). An academic scholar, Walzer, in the persuasion of Western philosophers seeks to universalize and objectivize considerations of value which, of course, cannot be done. Ethics, like theology, belongs to another realm—the realm of belief that carries different parameters of verification than does science.

Walzer's reading of the Just War heritage seeks to retain currency and political relevance to the principles and stipulates of the tradition. He rightly believes that global law administered through world courts is the best hope for a war-weary, beleaguered humanity. He affirms the following principles and practices, fine-tuned in historical experience:

- the rights of peoples to freedom and protection
- sovereignty and authority
- the right of mutual protection (alliances)
- military necessity (killing) and non-combatant immunity
- the rights of prisoners
- rules for terrorism, assassinations and reprisals
- supreme emergency
- deterrence
- punishment of war crimes

Paul Ramsey

Walzer takes issue with his Princeton colleague, my teacher, Paul Ramsey, when he deals with the issue of deterrence and all out war in a nuclear age. This discussion takes us to another reading on the normative position, which I offer. Visiting Ramsey's perspectives shows different theological premises than we generally find in secular "just-war" thought. A classic Christian thinker, rooted in the heritage of Augustine, Luther, Calvin, Barth and Niebuhr, Ramsey presents traditional views of issues such as the persistence of evil, the remediability of human violence, moral responsibility and the possibility of forgiveness and the capacity for Utopian construction. Though Ramsey's thought is traditional, his rhetoric always shows unusual erudition and fine-grained analysis.

Ramsey has been seen along with Reinhold Niebuhr as the most strenuous voice for Christian realism in twentieth century ethics. This becomes clear in his debate with Michael Walzer over nuclear deterrence. Ramsey argues that the threat of nuclear retaliation should be held over those who pose nuclear attack. This position goes against the flow of most late century philosophers. Walzer rejects the notion of deterrence and sees absolute suicidal futility in the use of nuclear weapons. He first summarizes Ramsey's view:

> Ramsey (I think of) as a Protestant soldier in a different tradition (from the pacifist). He has sought to establish a justifiable version of nuclear just war. "...He would have Americans gird themselves for a long continuous struggle with the forces of evil" (*Just and Unjust Wars*, p. 279).

Walzer holds a more skeptical realism:

> ...Nuclear weapons explode the theory of just war. They are the first of mankind's technological innovations that are simply not encompassable within the familiar moral world. ...our familiar notions about *jus in bello* require us to condemn even the threat to use them (p. 282).

Ramsey's view is in concord with my thesis in that it holds that war is sometimes necessary, just, and good in the confrontation with intractable evil (this must not be confused with President Bush's "axis of evil"). The suffering and sacrifice of the Jews, the German peoples, the Russian army and citizens, the Allies, the American fatalities and wounded, all against Hitler, were not absurd. Their sacrifice has been woven into a redemptive pattern of new life for the world. These died decalogically—akedically—for the Name and Way of God. The decades of

Afghan suffering, the loss of innocents from Pan Am flight 103 (1988), the bombing of African embassies, the ship "Cole," the victims of the World Trade Center, Pentagon and Pennsylvania, all contribute martyr deaths to the receipt of righteousness against the evils of bin Laden, Al Qaeda and the Western neglect, pretension and injustice which contributed to these evils. Part of the evil to be combated is Western violence against Muslims which fuels the Mujahadin martyrial ideologies, the Madrasas, and has provoked their fanatic, fulminating hatred. I affirm with Ramsey the necessity and efficacy of hard love, hard justice, hard forgiveness, and hard restitution.

I also affirm with Walzer that the deep respect for the integrity of the war convention makes absurd a limited, innocent, casualty-free nuclear strike. Posturing with such threats, especially from the only nation that has used nuclear weapons on civilians, is morally suspect. I have learned from Paul Ramsey, along with my teacher Helmut Thielicke and Ramsey's students Gil Meilander, Bill May and others, that the inner ethical meaning of war, in part, has to do with the mystery of suffering and sacrifice. The Hymn of Henry Wadsworth Longfellow contemplates this mystery:

I Heard the Bells on Christmas Day

> I heard the bells on Christmas day their old familiar carols play,
> And wild and sweet the words repeat of peace on earth, goodwill
>   to men.
> I thought how, as the day had come, the belfries of all Christendom
> Had rolled along th' unbroken song of peace on earth, goodwill to
>   men.
> And in despair I bowed my head: "There is no peace on earth," I
>   said,
> "For hate is strong, and mocks the song of peace on earth, goodwill
>   to men."
> Then pealed the bells more loud and deep, "God is not dead: nor
>   doth He sleep;
> The wrong shall fail, the right prevail, with peace on earth,
>   goodwill to men."

To be viewed honestly and circumspectly, war must be seen in the perspective of etiology and eschatology—of beginnings and endings. Even Just War theory views particular war causation and conduct in terms of the overarching and undergirding purview of justice and peace.

Walzer also directs our solemn attention to this long view:

> The dream of a war to end war, the myth of Armageddon, the
> vision of the lion lying down with the lamb—all these point toward

an age definitively peaceful, a distant age that lies across some unknown time-break, without armed struggle and symptomatic killing. ...Those of us trapped within that (intermediate) history have no choice but to fight on, defending the values to which we are committed... (*Just and Unjust Wars*, p. 329).

War is apocalyptic in nature. In biblical imagery it is one of the four horsemen, the ultimate specter of evil. Secular conventions and policies must of course deal with policies and practicalities. It must also comprehend this gravity and terror, this abhorrence and hope. Two great Christmastide texts convey this profound weight of our subject:

'Peace upon earth!' was said: We sing it,
And pay a million priests to bring it.
After two thousand years of mass
We've got as far as poison-gas.
Thomas Hardy, 'Christmas: 1924'

Ring out the want, the care, the sin,
The faithless coldness of the times;
Ring out, ring out my mournful rhymes,
But ring the fuller minstrel in.

Ring out false pride in place and blood,
The civic slander and the spite;
Ring in the love of truth and right,
Ring in the common love of good.

Ring out old shapes of foul disease,
Ring out the narrowing lust of gold;
Ring out the thousand wars of old
Ring in the thousand years of peace.

Ring in the valiant man and free,
The larger heart, the kindlier hand;
Ring out the darkness of the land,
Ring in the Christ that is to be.
Alfred Lord Tennyson, 'Christmas and New Year Bells'

To conclude the introduction and transition to our first chapter on the war on terrorism, let us reflect on the current situation.

As Christmastide, Jewish New Year and Ramadan, all Abrahamic holy days, settled in the second year of a new Christian millennium, a videotape of Osama bin Laden, "the arch Satan embodiment of evil" (George Bush) or "a prophetic voice" (Edward Said), was found at a house in Julalabad, Afghanistan. The transcript was chilling:

> Osama bin Laden converses with a Mullah, believed to be Ali Saeed al-Ghamdi, a former theology instructor at Umm al Qurrah Seminary in Mecca. (Transcription in *Newsweek*, December 24, 2001, p. 14).

> ASG: Everybody praises what you did, the great action you did, which was first and foremost by the grace of Allah. This is the guidance of Allah and the blessed fruit of Jihad. ...Sheik Suleyman Ulwan gave the *fatwa* on the Quran radio station he said..." This was jihad and those people (victims in World Trade Center and Pentagon) were not innocent. He swore to Allah.
> OBL: We calculated in advance the number of casualties from the enemy who would be killed based on the position of the tower. We calculated that the floors that would be hit would be three or four floors. ...due to my experience in this field, I was thinking that the fire from the gas in the plane would melt the iron structure of the building and collapse the area where the plane hit and all the floors above it only.
> ASG: A plane crashing into a tall building was out of anyone's imagination. This was a great job. He was a pious man, a martyr—Allah bless his soul.

On the videotape a subtitle read: "In revenge for the children of Al Aqsa (the children throwing stones on prayers at the wailing wall on whom Israeli soldiers opened fire killing 19.) ...Osama bin Laden executes an operation against America." (*Newsweek*, p. 15)

The mood across the Christian world this Advent-Christmastide-Epiphany is best described as an intense passion for justice and peace. The despicable treachery of Al Qaeda unleashed in Saudi Arabia, Kenya, Tanzania, Yemen and New York must be firmly repudiated and the planners and perpetrators brought to justice. One who has settled his research and conviction in Abrahamic faith and ethics can only wish that a global Islamic court would issue a *fatwa* condemning unholy suicidal terror, condemning in the same breath the unholy pride and materialism of the West which has provoked this aberration of peace (Islam).

Then the war for peace might ensue—"The War of the Lamb." John Howard Yoder, reflecting on the complex Revelation texts: "...Worthy is the lamb that was slain to receive power," (5:12). He finds this "not an inscrutable paradox but a meaningful affirmation."

...The cross and not the sword, suffering and not brute power determines the meaning of history" (*The Politics of Jesus*, Grand Rapids, Michigan: Eerdmans, 1972, p. 238).

So in the end *akedah*, grounded in decalogue not strategy grounded in power will win the war of the worlds.

2
The war on terrorism

In commending patience, forbearance in love and forgiveness, Yoder invokes the searching impulses of a powerful tradition of war/peace ethics called pacifism. Yet peace is elusive. Can it be that the final war will be like the final peace? The war on terrorism declared September 11 by America and by enthusiastic and reluctant allies seems hauntingly strange. It is framed in apocalyptic rhetoric:

- "Those not for us are against us."
- "Those who harbor terrorists are terrorists."

Look at what we face:

- A war with no tangible and defined enemy; rather a ubiquitous, antagonistic presence in cells around the world, supported by some 60 million people worldwide, according to Bush administration estimates: Hamburg, London, Islamabad, Miami, Newark, Detroit.
- A passionate animosity which spurs the true believers to gang violence and murder.
- A puritanical zeal which feels compelled to rid the world (or at least *dar al Islam*—Mecca, Medinah, Saudi Arabia) of the impurity of Western (American and Israeli) idolatry and immorality (a cleansing which we may also affirm).
- The war of ultimate power and nuance must have no casualties.

But this is not slogging trench warfare of Verdun with mustard gas wafting through the cold moist air. Now anthrax powder stirs in envelopes mailed to Senate office buildings. This is not the Enola Gay discharging her massive fission bombs over Nagasaki or Jimmy Doolittle's revenge raining fire-flak over Tokyo—revenge for Pearl Harbor I. Now it is Pearl Harbor II. It is earthquaking Big Berthas which send subterranean shockwaves for a ten-mile radius. It is box cutters stashed in Adidas bags and TATP plastic explosives molded in a man's basketball shoe.

Underneath, the war on terrorism is a crisis of conviction and commitment—a theological crisis. The crisis is as old as the call of Abraham. The crisis begins with the *hegira* and *akedah* of Abraham. It culminates in the "war of the lamb" where earthly power and conquest is renounced in favor of patient (suffering) righteousness. Scholars now see the book of Revelation as a text crafted in *Dekalogische Struktur*. This Abraham's biblical moral charter becomes the archaic and eschatic push and pull of international law, Nuremberg codes, Geneva Conventions, War Crimes Tribunals, just war theory, law of the Seas, global human rights conventions and all such peace and justice orders. This theological crisis, so cognizant of beginnings and endings, but also so contemporary, what Quakers and Peace churches such as Yoder's Mennonites call the "war of the lamb," is depicted in Volume II of Jack Miles, Pulitzer Prize winning theology, "Christ" (*CHRIST: A Crisis in the Life of God*, New York: Knopf, 2001).

In *GOD: A Biography* (New York: Knopf, 1995) Miles claimed that at the end of the Hebrew Bible God had fallen silent. The Natzorite refugees from Babylonian exile which included Mary and Joseph's families from Nazareth had waited long centuries for a king, a prophet, an anointed *Mesha*, a liberator to arise.

"A star shall come out of Jacob and a scepter out of Israel."
(Numbers 24:17)

In Christ God, says Miles with his relentless search for the character or the Actor God, now resolves this inner contradiction of God's self (omnipotent but helpless) by taking human form in his own Son and allowing the terror of the Roman Empire to execute him.

Miles' Christ centers on the akedic pivot of scripture, John 3:16:

"God so loved the world that he gave his only begotten (beloved) son (*monogenos, agapetos*) that whosoever believes in him shall not perish but have everlasting life."

To quote Miles in the context of Michael Wood's review (("Nobody's Perfect," review of *CHRIST: A Crisis in the Life of God*, New York: Knopf, 2001 in *NY Times Book Review*, December 23, 2001 p.8):

The not-yet Christian God, Miles suggests "needs a way to fail" and makes "a brilliant adjustment of the idea of the covenant," deciding to accept his own guilt for what has happened in the creation and to die for his people rather than scatter their human enemies once again. (Deuteronomic theodicy of war: my addition).

A priest who is his own sacrificial lamb, a lamb who is his own sacrificing priest, a father who is his own son, an Isaac who is his own Abraham, with the dagger in his own hand—it is by this fusion of identities that the crisis in the life of God is resolved.

...God by...becoming a Jew himself, Christ...swallows up the historical defeat of the Jews...(and) offers the promise of a cosmic victory that will "wipe away every tear" for all mankind" (from *CHRIST...*, jacket note).

How does this theological crisis help us comprehend the war on terrorism? I will argue in this book that the war of ancient Israel/Judea for Yahweh's presence on earth in late Bronze age Canaan then the Maccabean resistance culminating in the Roman Shoah against the Jews in Palestine (150 BCE to 150 CE) is paradigmatic to all Holy War. In a later chapter I will explore the tragic trifurcation of Abrahamic faith which becomes a contributory factor to that war.
　　Andrew Sullivan begins

The Osama bin Ladens of the world (and the orthodox fanatics in Israel and the fervent fundamentalists in America [my addition] – like the leaders of the Inquisition and others before and after them—demand that all embrace absolute faith. Individual faith and pluralism (not risky faith in a wounded, vulnerable God [my addition]) were the targets September 11, and it was only the beginning of an epic battle.
("This is a Religious War," *The New York Times Magazine*, October 7, 20001, p. 44)

Sullivan's essay is the best piece I know dealing with the currents of meaning in the war on terrorism. Though my judgment of the war on terrorism is at variance with Sullivan on crucial points, I believe that he strikes the correct chords. After several preliminary observations I will survey the theological and ethical meanings of the war "of" terrorism and "on" terrorism using the template of the Ten Commandments, bringing into dialogue three views: that of Al Qaeda, of Sullivan and my own.

The inner contradictions of Abrahamic religion
Soren Kierkegaard's *Fear and Trembling* traces the fundamental paradox in monotheism as expressed in the *visio dei* call, *HEGIRA* and *AKEDAH* of

Abraham. That one should be singled out, summoned and led to become forerunner in faith, whose progeny will be "as the stars of the sky and sands of the seashore" (Genesis 11) is preposterous and pretentious. This paradoxical nexus of faith entailing chosenness yet unworthiness (sacrifice), audacious power yet impotence, constitutes the basis of what will become the ambiguous witness of the Abraham seed-faiths as they dispense an admixture of violence and peace into the world. Jewish testimony, Christian evangelical announcement and Islamic devotion all have the bright side of justice and irenic gift and the dark side of faithless, fearful, violent persecution.

Of Islam for example which commends toleration, hospitality and love as well as coercion, Bernard Lewis says:

> There is something in the religious culture of Islam which inspired, in even the humblest peasant or peddler, a dignity and a courtesy toward others never exceeded and rarely equaled in other civilizations. And yet, in moments of upheaval and disruption, when the deeper passions are stirred, the dignity and courtesy toward others can give way to an explosive mixture of rage and hatred which impels even the government of an ancient and civilized country—even the spokesman of a great spiritual and ethical religion—to espouse kidnapping and assassination, (C-8, C-6) and try to find, in the life of their prophet, approval and indeed precedent for such actions (Lewis, quoted in Sullivan, p. 45).

The thesis we continue to develop in the chapter on the war on terrorism is that legitimate contention engenders justice, forgiveness and peace, while terrorism and war ensue in the illegitimate and aberrant strife of waning faith. Lewis argues that violence and terrorism are provoked in anomalous conditions of stress, anxiety, threat and humiliation. He confirms the Augustinian truth evidenced in domestic life that love and hate proceed from the same source. Under threat (terror) amity becomes animosity. This dialectic is frames by the great "Thou shall," "Thou shall not" of the Decalogue.

Commandments 1-3
Sullivan again quotes Lewis who goes to the heart of the intolerance and belligerence that is ill-founded adherence to the first commands. The ideological groundwork of the Madrasas (Koran Schools) and the Al Qaeda liturgy is that idolatry and blasphemy threaten the home of God (Allah) in the world. Diaries and documents found in Afghan caves tell of pledges to "kill the apostate" (violations of the imperative to believe – C1). The ideology makes two grievous mistakes: (1) it identifies the two parental

and sibling Abrahamic faiths as sources of this atheism denouncing the reality that they confess the same name (C-3). (2) Rather than trusting the divine will and God's judgment in history it takes the duty of fidelity and purification into its own hands then yields that responsibility into the corrupt hands of its own political movements: Taliban, Al Qaeda, Hamas, Egyptian Jihad, etc. Yet we agree that domination by a heretical Western faith based on money, power, materialism and secularism is an abomination. Sullivan phrases radical Islam's view:

> ...What is truly evil and unacceptable is the domination of infidels over true believers. For true believers to rule misbelievers is proper and natural, since this provides for the maintenance of the Holy law and gives the misbelievers both the opportunity and the incentive to embrace the true faith. But for misbelievers to rule over true believers is blasphemous and unnatural, since it leads to the corruption of religion and morality in society and to the flouting or even the abrogation of God's law (Sullivan, p. 52).

Since the days when America first undermined the Muslim fabric of life in Iran in the 1950's and 60's and propped up the secularist Shah who sponsored the worst of Western values, we have contributed to this conspiratorial theology which marked the regime of Ayatollah Khomeini and other passionate religious Muslims in the lands of Arabia. Our endorsement, even fabrication of quasi-secular regimes throughout the region, regimes which opposed both Islamic fervor, and the imposition of Shariah as legal system on the one hand and human rights and participatory democracy on the other, all in our craving for cheap oil and political hegemony, was also a mistaken public policy and an erroneous reading of the theological ethic of the first (God-adherence) commandments.

One caveat. I believe that part of the appropriate theological destiny of America and the Christian West in world history is the extension of economic opportunity and prosperity into impoverished areas. I celebrate President Bush's call on January 2002 (State of the Union Address) for a "freedom corps" and an amplified Peace Corps to send thousands of volunteers into the needy world to, as he says, "love the children"—to educate children, shelter the homeless, heal the sick, clothe the naked, liberate the oppressed and bring good news to the poor. While my theology is strongly critical of substitutionary materialism for devotion to God alone, I believe that a particular burden of our history (through the Anglican and Puritan faith history) is to generate wealth in the world, to stimulate its entrepreneurial ethos and distribute that derivative wealth equitably. John Calvin's ethic of the rich and the poor is to give back and to share. If this is the case then part of the spiritual and ethical vocation of the West is to challenge the hoarding and concentrating of wealth both in America and Arabia. We need to rephrase both the radical Islamic and pagan Western construals of economic vocation. Equal and just economic opportunity requires, as another important war theorist George Landes, *The Wealth and Poverty of Nations*, says, both freedom and socially responsible policies of taxation and wealth distribution.

Osama bin Laden saw the war as strife against "unbelief and unbelievers." The Taliban's destruction of the colossal ancient Buddhas was a symptom of an iconoclasm which reminds one of Jewish iconoclasm against Hellenic monuments, early Christian destruction of Greco-Roman temples and statuary, the Crusaders trashing, even of Hagia Sophia-Constantine's church in Istanbul, Islam's sometime virulent destruction of Christian sites and Henry VIII's then the Puritan's destruction of the beauty of England's lovely cathedrals.

The issue of iconoclasm is complex. In rigorous Semitic sensibility any artifactual simulation of the divine is suspect. It could be argued in terms of radical irreplicability mimesis that not only buildings and statues, sanctuaries and scriptures, but even theological texts are human constructs and therefore incapable of bearing the divine. Iconoclasm in this sense may be a preservation of the integrity of the divine. Nothing penultimate ought to be invested with divinity (*Finitum non capax infiniti*). The dilemma of this view is that the iconoclast himself presumes the veracity and divine authority of his own construal of the truth and of his own designation of the other as inferior and "corrupt."

"Defending the faith" has proven historically to be the prime religious value in offensive and defensive war. "To insure a home for the divine presence (name)" is the essence of Israel's Holy War in first millennium BC Canaan. That the "Name of Christ" not be obliterated from the earth animates the Crusades, especially the campaign against Jerusalem (securing Constantine's and Helen's churches including the Holy Sepulcher in Jerusalem and the Church of the Nativity in Bethlehem). Osama bin Laden's December 2001 tape heralds the "Blessed terrorism" of the period surrounding 9/11 as contesting "the crusade of America and Israel against Islam." In the Reformation and in the religious wars and Cousins' Wars this C 1-3 value is expressed as demand for religious freedom. Across the millennia thousands have died that "the Gospel be preached and lived."

The dilemma surrounding the God-war commands (C1-3) is finally the quandary of modernity/post-modernity. Is there objective and universal reality and truth or do we only have relativity and refracted insight (what Plato called *doxa* - opinion). Sullivan calls for a theological and ethical reserve which decries:

...The blind recourse to texts embraced as literal truth, the injunction to follow the commandments of God before anything else, the subjugation of reason and judgment and even conscience to the dictates of dogma... (those who) believe that there is an eternal afterlife and that endless indescribable torture awaits those who disobey God's laws... (those who) make sure that you not only conform to each Diktat but that you also encourage and, if necessary coerce others to do the same. Sin begets sin, the sin of others can corrupt you (46).

Sullivan's indictment obviously, is fulminant Enlightenment liberalism. There can be no truth or right—only reservation and relativity.

Actually the theological commands establish a very delicate equipoise—one between truth and pretension. God alone is truth and good. Nothing else, certainly not human persuasion, can be imbued with those qualities. While faith is rightly grounded adherence to dogma or belief, dogmatism and skepticism go hand in hand. Faith alone can ground humility. Arrogance which issues in aggression is actually disguised and projected agnosticism. Terrorism is the absence of faith or more properly the violent counter-reaction of those struggling to believe against doctrinaire unbelief. Such idolatrous secularity is too often the god portrayed by the Christian West.

A final note about the First Commandment, "No Other Gods." This prime value of all existence exists in universal piety which precedes the advent of high religion. Grounded then in Abraham's election and Israel's exodus, liberation and constitution, the first command becomes the source of human freedom. This value is amplified in culture through the influence of the philosophy and political law of classical Greece (see V. Hanson, *Carnage and Culture*). If God alone is Lord of the soul and master of the conscience, no other tyranny or rule can stand. As Barth, Niemoller and Bonhoeffer would shout against the Nazi self-deification, "Gott ist mein Führer." This charter of freedom is deeply embedded in Abrahamic consciousness and obedience as well as in the faith assertions of the three Abrahamic faiths.

Again we find here a very controversial political philosophy and economic school proceeding from the faith. An historical example: The Scots Convenanters in the Seventeenth Century, like the Somerset non-conformists before them and the American Patriots to follow, are "freedom fighters" against the political and ecclesial establishment. Those who are labeled "terrorists" by their antagonists are usually called "freedom fighters" by their advocates and apologists. Che Guevara in Cuba and South America, Mao Tse Tung in China, and Ho Chi Minh in Viet Nam are throwbacks, even sometimes protégés of the American and French revolutionaries.

Walzer finds Guerillas and freedom fighters as part of the noble heritage of good war/just war patriots. Their excellence is sealed by their hatred of oppression, their love for the common people, their willingness to self-sacrifice. It is sullied by their too-easy violence. Only history can determine who among those who have been called terrorists—Menachem Begin, Anwar Sadat, Osama bin Laden, Colin Powell—are actually patriots.

Commandments 4-5

These commandments governing observance of the Sabbath, work and rest in general and familial piety, also impinge on the war of/on terrorism. In 1998 Osama bin Laden cried out against American violation of the Muslim sacred place and holy family.

> The call to wage war against America was made because America has spearheaded the crusade against the Islamic nation (family) sending tens of thousands of its troops to the land of the two holy mosques (Sabbath) over and above its meddling in its affairs and its politics and its support of the oppressive, corrupt and tyrannical (C-1) regime that is in control (Sullivan, p. 45).

Sacra familia, terra sancta, and sanctuary are complex doctrines in the Abraham faith communities. Your house of worship and home are to be inviolable citadels of faith, nurtured and protected with one's love, service, even life. Here faith, hope and love are born and transmitted. Yet these two doctrines also retain an ancient Bedouin element. Related to ancient near-Eastern hospitality, sanctuary requires the hosting and safeguarding of the stranger, sojourner, even the enemy. Obviously President Bush's indictment of harboring "terrorists" is problematic as was the policy of his father of "busting" American churches offering sanctuary to Nicaraguan exiles. In Bethlehem's Church of the Nativity and Christmas Lutheran, sanctuary has been violated by the Israeli incursion of April 2002.

The theological doctrine, ethical obligation and political duty of C 4 and 5 are born in the startling assertion "the earth is the Lord's" (Psalm 8). Defending the motherland is an impulse to sustain not only the microcosm of the family and tribe and the cosmos of the nation but the macrocosm of the wide world. The Abrahamic doctrine at stake is "angels unawares" (Hebrews 13:2). In receiving the visitor one entertains God disguised as the neighbor.

> When did we see you hungry and feed you
> naked and clothed you

in prison and visited you?
In as much as you did it unto the least of my brethren
you did it to me…
(Matthew 25 after Egyptian funerary texts)

Just as America's finest destiny is opening itself up, Emma Lazarus-wise, to
the "tired and poor, huddled masses yearning to breathe free," all nations of
the world in *dar al Islam*, in Christendom and in *'aretz Israel* must be
havens and hostels to the diverse families of the world. This is the epitome
and epiphany of Abraham's faith enfolding "all nations of the world."

Commandment 6

To ignore or flaunt divine and natural law by asserting superiority over it or
unwillingness to submit to it by reason of power, sovereignty or authority
over it, strikes fear into the heart of others. To breach such instruction
(Torah) is to menace others. To kill, rape and pillage is to terrify the world.
This section of our exploration of the war on terrorism is the most difficult.
Its theme is the most subtle and nuanced. To kill in war and under threat
involves profound issues such as:

- killing civilians (either collaterally or intentionally)
- assassination
- combat mortality itself

Let us explore the morality of these issues within the current context.
    Initially we must note a sequentialism implied in the unfolding of our
thesis. Basic to the modes of moral law and ethical principles of the
Abrahamic tradition (Torah, Christian ethics, Shi'rah), is the process and
momentum that proceeds from thought to will to act. The biblical
transaction flows in this way:

- "the fruit was pleasant to the eye"
- "the serpent beguiled me"
- "I ate it"

Similarly with killing, meditation precedes intention which proceeds to
action. When Madrasas (Koran Schools) in Afghanistan and Pakistan
enjoin suicide-assassination as Holy Law they violate this cardinal
command of Allah.
    Though initially each Abrahamic faith movement (*hegira*) involves
terror, violence and killing, both defensively and offensively, to protect and
establish the faith, the movements are deeply and normatively more irenic
than bellic. The "conquest" in Canaan probably was no such thing and we

know that even though Solomon's realm could have been an empire, it settles into a provincial kingdom. Like Moses, Jesus' appearance in the world is accompanied by infanticide. (Exodus 2:15, 12, Matthew 2:12) The early church is so dispossessed of this world that even three centuries after apostolic times, Constantine's state, even to Augustine, verges on pagan audacity. Though Mohammed's *hegira* begins with the sword, ostensibly to protect the nascent revelation, his final trek to Mecca is weaponless, placing himself at the mercy of his adversaries.

Despite this peaceful norm at the center of the three faiths, crises and threats seem to turn the embracing political structure and even the faith movements themselves hostile and violent. In the 1930's a tendency emerged in Islam which turned many persons—Mullahs and zealous laymen—radical and aggressive. In 1948-50 Israel is planted in Palestine and America overturns Mohammed Mozedeh in Iran and plants the Shah. In Egypt in the 1950's and 60's the radicals were jailed, tortured and executed in their homes for their venom against Western influence and their desire to replace their regimes with Islamic states. These extremists like the Egyptian Jihad in 1981 assassinated President Anwar Sadat, whom the West saw as a new peace and justice Pharaoh. (Throughout this section I am indebted to the essay by Robert Worth, "Justifying Murder: The Deep Intellectual Roots of Islamic Terror" *The New York Times*, October 13, 2001, p. A 13, 15).

A document found after that stadium massacre which killed Sadat called "The Neglected Duty" provided theological justification for suicidal assassination because rulers had abandoned Islam. Like some Puritan documents (even the American Declaration of Independence: "The people have the right and duty to abolish that government"), tyrannicide was justified as duty to God and the people.

Al Qaeda emerges out of the Islamic Jihad movements which spring up in the 1980's and 1990's throughout the Middle East and Western Asia. Osama bin Laden's world view finds even deeper resource in a version of otherwise liberal and magnanimous medieval Islam which had turned defensive against the Spanish Inquisition and Mongol hegemony. *Salafiyya* sought to purify Islam to its seventh-century origins from the corruptions of idolatry. It must be remembered that both Judaism and Mohammedism have a strong anti-idolatry tenor in their origins. Like Israel before and Islam after, Christianity is a movement to purify YAHWEH faith from an "idolatrous and adulterous generation." (Mark 12:39) The official Wahhabi ideology of Saudi Arabia is this version of purging, Puritan cleansing, restoration and strict adherence. Regrettably the Saudi and other affluent Emirites which adopted this theocratic program missed its prophetic fury against injustice and neglect of the poor.

Major literary influences on radical Islamic Jihad, Al Qaeda and Osama bin Laden were Sayyid Qutb who wrote *Signposts on the Road* (1964) and Abdallah Azam, a Palestinian who was killed by a car bomb in 1989. Such thinkers influenced the former rich Saudi playboy by transforming the Islamic stipulate against killing a fellow Muslim, now finding it acceptable, even honorable to kill them if they were Jews, Christians or pseudo-Muslims. The thought forwarded was that an official within *dar-al-Islam* who is not Muslim is a positive threat to social and spiritual integrity in the nation.

Muhammad Johrat Husain writes concerning the ethical justifications for physical *jihad* (strife) and *quital* (combat):

> ...Jihad means struggle, striving in the cause of Allah and includes killing and being killed in his way.
> In Koran *Jihad* is mentioned 28 times, *quital* 34 times, e.g., "...fight in... Allah's cause against those who wage war against you" (but do not commit aggression) "...slay them whenever you come upon them" "...fight against them until there is no more oppression and all worship is devoted to Allah alone" (2: 190-193).

The main theme of the killing document of Hussain is that killing is authorized by the presence of oppression (*fitna*). The major difficulty already evident is that liberty-grounded peoples like America and Israel do not think of their presence or influence in cultural phenomena like secularism, democracy and capitalism as oppression. So we continue. For Hussein's reading of Koran, oppression is "worse than killing." "While killing is evil, yet it is enjoined to crush a bigger evil." Here we have a utilitarian addendum to the actual command "do not kill."

Finally, there is reward for killing oppressors. "Those who sacrifice their lives for the cause of Allah get an exalted eternal life immediately, and are called martyrs (*shaheed*)." ("Two Views: Can the Koran Condone Terror?", *New York Times*, October 13, 2001, p. A 15).

The argument of justifiable homicide at the political and theological level remains problematic. Was the judicial murder of King Charles I (1649) by the Puritans warranted? Were the conspirators in the aborted July 20, 1944 movement to assassinate Adolf Hitler justified? Bonhoeffer, Dohnanyi and my teacher, Helmut Thielicke, struggled with this issue. It is the same genre of issue as the justification of the instant killing of 100,000+ Japanese civilians with the atomic bombs at Hiroshima and Nagasaki. Does the greater good of end of war (Truman) or relief of oppression (bin Laden) justify the killings?

The persuasion of the particular thesis I am putting forward is that these acts of so called "redeeming death" are not justified. For two reasons: (1)

the ethic rooted in the reality of God reserves life and death dealing to God alone. From human calculations such acts may seem to be good and helpful. But in the divine purview, which sees beyond the exigencies of the moment and of human passions, all killing is blasphemous and evil. (2) Secondly, even in terms of human consequences such acts always set in motion a cycle of reprisals. Osama bin Laden's first videotape mentioned one American atrocity in particular—the nuclear bombing of Japanese civilians at Hiroshima and Nagasaki. In biblical ethics a killing must be commanded by God. All other killing is outlawed. The philosophical justification of homicide in capital punishment, war, self defense and abortion are rational but theologically sinful. God's call to Abraham to offer Isaac is the paradigm. If righteous and moral war, say of the U.S. Civil War against slavery or WWII against Hitler is justified, that justification provides allowances for killing, though it remains full of remorse and repentance.

In addition to this theological and pragmatic premise our thesis adds yet another dimension which forbids intentional killing. Joining *akedah* to Abraham in the moral structure of reality argues that salvific (redemptive) death has occurred with finality in the being of God. The meaning of Messiah (The Anointed One) in Hebrew and Christian faith and of the sacrificial lamb in all three expressions of the heritage is that the sin of the world and the burden of righteous recompense (judgment) has ultimately become a divine act. There is no longer necessity for humans to take justice in matters of life and death into their own hands. We will develop the meanings of this, albeit marginal thesis, as we go along, especially with further reference to Jack Miles, *CHRIST*.... For now we note that the sublime metaphysical and eschatological realities of forgiveness and peace militate against the necessity of terrorism and war. Realism vis-à-vis the enduring stupidity and violence of humanity will always counter-mitigate this transcending reality, offering the remote possibility of a holy passion of justice.

The New York Times Essay carrying Muhammed Husain's document also contains an excerpt from an article by Prof. Bernard Haykel, a professor of Islamic law at New York University. He concludes:

According to Islamic law there are at least six reasons why bin Laden's barbaric violence cannot fall under the rubric of jihad: (1) Individuals and organizations cannot declare a jihad, only states can. (2) One cannot kill innocent women and children when conducing a jihad. (3) One cannot kill Muslims in a jihad. (4) One cannot fight a jihad against a country in which Muslims can freely practice their religion and proselytize Islam. (5) Prominent Muslim jurists around the world have condemned these attacks, and their condemnation forms a juristic consensus (*ijma*) against bin Laden's actions. This consensus renders his actions un-Islamic. (6) The welfare and interest of the Muslim community (*mas-laha*) is being harmed by bin Laden's actions and this equally makes them un-Islamic (A15).

Commandment 7
Seeing the ubiquitous "corn-flower blue" burqah reminds us that concerns of women, sexuality and family life are also central to the war on terrorism. A quotation from Sayyid Qutb reveals this dimension of the insult and the response. Working as a literary critic between 1948 and 1950 in the U.S., even in those pious and puritan days at the dawn of the Eisenhower years, he documents his disgust at the Kinsey Report and the degradation caused by the thought of Darwin, Marx and Freud on Western consciousness and conscience: "...no one is more distant than the Americans from spirituality and piety" (p. A15).

He also described the sexual promiscuity with what I remember as a typical (Methodist and Presbyterian) church dance of the 1950's; this particular example took place in Greeley, Colorado:

> ...Every young man took the hand of a young woman. And these were young men and women who had just been singing their hymns. Red and blue lights, with only a few white lamps, illuminated the dance floor. The room became a confusion of feet and legs: arms twisted around hips; lips met lips; chests pressed against chests (p. A15).

This shocked description of the 50's youth culture is very close to that offered by their own Methodist and Presbyterian parents. Nor is it far from the proscribed and prescribed sexual behaviors in Ayatollah Khomeini's Iran or the strict love, sex, dating and female behavioral ethics of the Taliban in Afghanistan. Here girls could not go to school or work outside the home. Medical care for women was wanting. The full burqah and robe concealed the beauty of the female body from the ever-temptable Muslim male. While Islamic sexual ethics are a subject beyond the scope of this book on war, the theme does contribute to our topic and to the controversy surrounding the American led war of liberation. Was the freedom of the "American Way" which we espoused really an advocacy of sexual license and promiscuity?

One small footnote: During the Afghanistan campaign a contradiction caught my eye. I noted in my journal that the Afghans will now again be able to grow poppy and supply the West's insatiable appetite for drugs once the Taliban's pharmacologic Puritanism is past, (they had nearly eliminated the poppy fields). One wonders if we will see the same kind of mingled liberation/degradation that we witnessed with the collapse of communism in Eastern Europe. Yes, state tyranny and bureaucracy was gone. No more state-provided work, education, health care, proscribed behavior, etc. But now the diseases of Western affluence would take off and thrive: gun violence, drug abuse, gnawing poverty, uneven social services, homelessness. The few had Mercedes but a "do your own thing" indulgence was now rampant.

In biblical and Abrahamic ethics male and female are liberated to the joys and duties of family responsibility. We are now blessed between man and woman with a radical equality and reciprocal service. The nurture of children, the primary vocation of generations, is the sacred privilege conveyed in human love. The seventh commandment, the charter of sexual freedom, justice and care, casts a beam of critical judgment on both Taliban and MTV sex ethics.

As Oprah Winfrey declines the invitation of George Bush to visit the girls' school in Afghanistan, this observer questions Bush's new-found interest in women's liberation.

The secularized Christian world can learn from the Islamic world the virtues of modesty, chastity and fidelity. The Islamic world can learn of the liberty and diversity of conjugal relations from the Christian. Both learn from Judaism the covenants of deep care and joy in family life. For all three communities war and strife can yield to forgiveness and peace presenting a better world for all pathways of Abraham's family.

Responsibility in community is the goal of Abrahamic sexual morality. America should not rejoice in destroying Muslim family ethics. Islamic nations should exult in the freedom and opportunity for women, minorities, the poor and the outcast, that is the liberating moral legacy of the Abrahamic faith and life heritage.

Commandments 8-10

Seizure, piracy and *Landnahmen* (expropriation of territory) are implicit in the war of and against terrorism. Taliban wait at crossroads and seize parcels and belongings. They kidnap and kill Mr. Daniel Pearl, the reporter. Kidnapping is the central biblical meaning of the Eighth Command . The grand exploits of colonialism—first that of the Ottomans, then that of Europe and the West lie behind the war on terrorism. The sins of exploitation and expropriation are the sins of the final set of commandments in the Holy tableau. Stealing, deceiving and coveting are misdirected desire where persons and peoples fail to honor the property and possessions of one another. The craving of cheap oil to fuel the intemperate ambitions of the West has been a grave violation of the resources of others. The primal crime in the Gulf War is now recognized to be the American and the West's grasping envy of Gulf Oil and Kuwait's siphoning off of the oil field lying underneath Iraq and Kuwait.

The seizure of the country of Afghanistan by the Taliban was reprehensible as was the preceding ambition of the Soviet Union. The cumulative effect of little deceptions, envies, covetings and seizures has created a fabric of malice and danger. The gun-running, drug-trafficking, money-laundering and credentials—falsifying on all sides of the conflict has created a milieu of inhumanity and destruction. The betrayal, assassination, undermining of respect, war-lording and other violence has created an atmosphere where war and terrorism thrives and forgiveness and peace shrivels. Only a new day of equanimity and mutual affirmation can restore shalom to a war torn, rubble-strewn land like Afghanistan. In my comments after 9/11 I argued for a peace-corps to rebuild homes, clothe the naked, feed the hungry, heal the sick, educate the searchers, supply the needy. In shocked patriotic America that didn't preach.

Concrete policies and actions
The foregoing analysis of the theological, moral and political themes of the war on terrorism confirms the groundwork for a response of concrete action. Though he inexcusably denies the Armenian Genocide (*Le Monde*, November 13, 1993), we follow essentially the lines of Princeton professor Bernard Lewis ("Did You Say American Imperialism?", *National Review*, Dec. 17, 2001).

The underlying theological ambiguities noted in the family of Abrahamic faiths and sketched in their moral ramifications in the preceding section have led to a political uncertainty which has plagued national policies such as those of the U.S., England, France, Iraq, Saudi Arabia, Egypt, Pakistan and Israel. It has also given an uncertain trumpet call to international policies (e.g., UN, NATO, Council of Islamic Nations, etc.).

As we noted in our book *Ethics and the Gulf War* (Boulder: Westview, 1992) the Gulf War ended in the equivocal quandary of whether to displace the government of Saddam Hussein (as we did the Taliban government in Afghanistan) with all of the bloodshed, permanent occupation, etc., that such action would have required.

Lewis notes that in Iraq President George Bush, Sr. decided after 100 hours on the ground to end hostilities. This decision has been roundly criticized even though most of the studies of the ethics of the Gulf War opposed the coalition intervention, per se, and breathed a sigh of relief when the General MacArthur mania of going into China (now Baghdad) was rejected. Since coalition goals did not include the liberation of Iraq from "domestic tyranny" a policy of "off and on" protection of Kurds in the north, constant overflies, inspection of weapons of mass destruction manufacture and most regrettably embargo and sanctions has followed.

This enduring grievance has provided one of the Holy trinity of suicide-meriting objectives for Al Qaeda propaganda (the others being Israel/American occupation and oppression in Palestine and the U.S. military presence in *Terra Sancta*-Saudi Arabia).

Osama bin Laden's primary *casus belli* is that "American crusaders" have joined Israeli "Holy Warriors" to imperially impose their will on Arab Muslims and to introduce their corruptions, principally materialistic secularization on the Holy lands—*dar al Islam*. Actually American interests in the region are more pragmatic than effusively moral and theological, claims Lewis: "...the supply of oil and the survival of Israel" (27). These interests will continue to exacerbate wounds and will require humanitarian modification though they must be retained as firm commitments.

America's abortive incursion into Somalia was even more problematic. In 1993 and 1994 America was drawn into the warlord strife in this East African nation in the waning years of the Cold War. Getting close with troops and Blackhawk Helicopters she found herself with her sophisticated computerized war technology threatened by chaotic violence of gang warfare in a desperately poor no-man's land. Casualties were taken, indecision followed and the world's greatest and richest power turned timid and high-tailed it out of there.

The threat to world security and western interests was real and intense. Weapons of mass destruction had been used: by Nasser of Egypt against Yemen in the Sixties, by Qaddafi of Libya against Chad in 1987 and by Hussein and Iraq against Iran and even his own compatriots in 1988. Tens of thousands had been killed. Osama bin Laden, El Qaeda and ignorantly fervent and indoctrinated Arab Muslims misconstrued the complex history of Western, especially American response as the perpetuation of the Christian Crusades of the middle ages. Even though recent American interventions and sympathies in Somalia, Bosnia, Kosovo, even Chechnya were on the side of Muslims, the simplistic phobia prevailed. Thus the war of terrorism.

Now, in the aftermath of the checkmate of the venomous violence Lewis argues for a more thoughtful pattern of mid-east actions. Such policy in my view might include:

- Less dependence on oil in favor of cheaper, cleaner, more accessible sources of energy.
- Transcend the Arab/Israeli cold war machinations reenacting the "smile" confrontation long after the Russia/U.S. angry Cheshire cat is gone.
- Massive educational aid to the region so that ideologically violent Madrasas are not the only educational options in the region.

- Massive sharing of Western wealth especially to the poor of this region—including Africa and the poverty belt of Southern Asia—knowing that our extraction of oil and other resources has unjustly impoverished this region. Give back (C 8-10) to its owners.
- Most critically, the policy must be firm and formidable.

In a forceful summary in National Review essay in December (17) 2001, Lewis claims that "the range of American options in the Middle East is being reduced to two alternatives, both disagreeable: "Get tougher or get out" (p. 30). The full-fledged, theologically grounded proposal I offer is embodied in The Jerusalem Sabeel Document subtitled "Principles for a Just Peace in Palestine-Israel" (2000). If as I proposed early in this study, the Palestine-Israel conflict, its history and prospects, are the epicenter of the global war of/on terrorism then this charter may guide us safely forward.

Theological basis
Our faith teaches us that:
1. God, creator and redeemer, loves all people equally (John 3:16, Acts 17:24-28).
2. God demands that justice be done. No enduring peace, security, or reconciliation is possible without the foundation of justice. The demands of justice will not disappear; and the struggle for justice must be pursued diligently and persistently but non-violently (Jeremiah 9:23-24, Isaiah 32:16-17, Romans 12:17-21).
3. The Holy Land is God's gift to Palestinians and Israelis [to Jews, Christians and Muslims]. They must live justly and mercifully and be good stewards of it (Micah 6:8).
4. "Love your neighbor as yourself" is an inclusive principle that must be honored and sought after (Mark 12:31). The Golden Rule continues to apply, "Do to others what you want them to do to you" (Matthew 7:12).
5. Faithfulness to God obliges us to work for justice, peace, forgiveness, reconciliation, and healing (Matthew 5:9, 43-45).
6. [My amendment: It requires that we work against hatred, terrorism and war].

Moral basis
1. We acknowledge the sufferings and injustices committed against Jews by the West, especially those inflicted in the holocaust. Nevertheless, they do not justify the injustices committed against Palestinians. Justice claimed by one people at the expense of another is not justice.

2. Since Israel has, by force, displaced the Palestinians, destroyed their villages and towns, denied them their basic human rights and illegally dominated and oppressed them, it is morally bound to admit its injustice against the Palestinians and assume responsibility for it.
3. Since Israel acquired by force 77% of the land of Palestine in 1948, approximately 20% more than the Untied Nations had allotted, and established its state there, it is moral and right for Israel to return the whole of the areas captured in 1967, i.e. the Gaza Strip and West Bank, including East Jerusalem, to the millions of Palestinians who need their own small sovereign state.
4. Israel's 'Law of Return' which allows any Jewish person to immigrate to Israel while denying Palestinians the right of return to their homeland is immoral and discriminatory.
5. Sharing the sovereignty of Jerusalem [or declaring international sovereignty] is imperative to a moral and just peace.
6. The ideology of militarism as well as the stockpiling [or the surreptitious importing] of weapons of mass destruction [by either Israel or Palestine] is morally wrong. They sabotage the spirit and viability of peace and will not provide security either.

Legal basis: international legitimacy
The following principles have been affirmed and repeatedly reaffirmed by the international community.

1. Palestinian refugees have the right of return—UN General Assembly Resolution 194.
2. The Gaza Strip and the West Bank, including East Jerusalem, are occupied territories and the Israeli forces must withdraw from them—UN Security Council Resolution 242 and 338 based on the international principle of the inadmissibility of the acquisition of territory by force.
3. The Israeli settlements in the Gaza Strip and West Bank, including East Jerusalem are illegal. Moreover, it is illegal for the occupying power to transfer its population to, or to change the status of, the occupied territories—Fourth Geneva Convention.
4. East Jerusalem is occupied territory. Israel's unilateral actions to alter the status of Jerusalem are illegal and invalid—UN Security Council Resolutions 252 and 478.
5. Violations of human rights such as home demolitions, land confiscation, torture, revocation of residency rights, restriction of movement, closures, and the monopolization of resources are an insult to the dignity of human beings and contravene international law—Untied Nations Universal Declaration of Human Rights.

The principles which Sabeel stands for

The people of the region—Palestinians and Israelis—both need and deserve a lasting peace, and security. With peace and security in place, bonds of acceptance and friendship can grow. It is no service to either community to promote a peace which flouts international law, ignores justice, and ultimately cannot endure since this will lead to continued bitterness and violence.

The following principles are, therefore, based on international legitimacy. The international community has a responsibility to see that they are fulfilled. Once achieved, the strongest international guarantees must be given to ensure that the people of Palestine and Israel will live in peace and security.

1. Israel must admit that it has committed an injustice against the Palestinian people and must accept responsibility for that. This means that reparation must be paid to all Palestinians who have suffered as a result of the conflict since 1948 whether they are Palestinian citizens of Israel, Palestinians living on the West Bank and the Gaza Strip, or Palestinians living in the Diaspora. The road to healing and reconciliation passes through repentance, forgiveness and redress.

2. [Palestinians must acknowledge their persistent violence and sabotage against the Israeli people. The harm done to innocent civilians by terrorists and suicidal attacks is unconscionable requiring repentance, forgiveness and amendment of ways.]

3. The Palestinians must have their own sovereign, independent, and democratic state established on the whole of the Gaza Strip and West Bank, including East Jerusalem. Israel must withdraw to the June 4, 1967, borders. No solution is acceptable if it does not guarantee the Palestinians' and Israelis' right to self-determination, independence, and sovereignty.

4. Jerusalem's sovereignty must be shared by the two states of Palestine and Israel. The city must remain open for Palestinians, Israelis, and all. East Jerusalem can be the capital of Palestine while West Jerusalem can be the capital of Israel. Any agreement must protect the sanctity of the holy places and guarantee the rights of the three religions—Christianity, Islam, and Judaism—on an equal basis. All illegal confiscation of land or expansion of areas by Israel within the walled city of Jerusalem since 1967 must be reversed.

5. The right of return to Palestinian refugees must be guaranteed according to international law. All refuges must be fully compensated.

6. All Israeli Jewish settlements on the Gaza Strip and West Bank, including East Jerusalem, are illegal under international law. All the settlements built on Palestinian soil since 1967 must be part of Palestine.

7. Once the principles of an acceptable justice are applied, a peace treaty must be drawn up between the two states of Palestine and Israel guaranteeing the full sovereignty and territorial integrity of each including recognized borders, water rights, and other resources.

8. Furthermore, both states must fully guarantee the respect and protection of the human rights of all their citizens, including freedom of religion, in accordance with all international conventions.

Political background

In 1948 a grievous [though morally necessary] injustice was committed by the Zionists (forerunners of the state of Israel) against the Palestinian people. The Zionists acquired by force 77% of the land of Palestine and displaced three quarters of a million Palestinians. Consequently, the state of Israel was declared a Jewish state. Since then, most of the displaced Palestinians have lived in refugee camps and their national rights have been denied. Despite UN Resolution 194, passed in December 1948 and reaffirmed annually by the UN, Israel has adamantly refused the right of return of Palestinian refugees to their homes. The 150,000 Palestinians who remained within that part of Palestine which became the state of Israel were given Israeli citizenship. However, they have been discriminated against and treated as second class citizens.

In 1967, the state of Israel acquired by force the rest of the country of Palestine (the 23%) further displacing approximately 325,000 Palestinians. The Palestinians living in the Gaza Strip and the West Bank came under Israeli military rule. The occupation has been oppressive, brutal, and dehumanizing. Palestinian land has been systematically confiscated, human rights violated, and people systemically humiliated, as documented by a number of international, Israeli, and Palestinian human rights organizations, such as Amnesty International, B'Tselem, LAW and Al-Haq. Furthermore, Israel assumed control of Palestine's water supply (unfairly restricting water to Palestinians and charging them exorbitant prices), began building exclusively Jewish settlements on Palestinian land and, through hundreds of military laws, persisted in its oppression of the Palestinians.

As to East Jerusalem, Israel annexed it and, in 1993, closed it and cut it off from the rest of the West Bank and Gaza Strip, thus denying Palestinians the right of access to it. Consequently, even the right to worship in its churches and mosques is obstructed. Moreover, Israel enacted a policy to limit the Palestinian presence in Jerusalem to 27% of the city's population through demolition of homes, confiscation of land, revocation of Palestinian residency rights as well as other means.

In 1991 at the end of the Gulf War, the peace process was initiated by the United States and Russia. In spite of its initial promise in the Madrid Conference to achieve a just peace, it became, in its Oslo form, an instrument for furthering the injustice. As it evolved, certain portions of the occupied territories were returned by Israel to the Palestinian Authority. By the end of March 2000, only 18.2% of the area of the West Bank has been returned to full Palestinian Authority; 24.7% is under Israeli security and Palestinian civil control. The remaining 57.1% of the West Bank is still under full Israeli control. The areas that have been returned to the Palestinians are not geographically linked together. The Israeli Army controls the highways and major roads throughout the occupied territories, as well as everything below the ground and sky above. It is important to note that in the Gaza Strip, only 60% of the land is under Palestinian control where over a million Palestinians live; while Israel controls the 40% of the Strip for the benefit of 6100 Jewish settlers. Furthermore, some of the 194 Israeli settlements (166 in the West Bank and Gaza Strip and 28 in East Jerusalem—all illegal under international law—have expanded to sizable towns. It is estimated that the number of settlers, including those who live in the settlement ring in and around Jerusalem, is approximately 400,000.

The two sides, Israelis and Palestinians, have more recently been engaged in the final status negotiations which include the thorniest issues, namely, Jerusalem, borders, refugees, water, and settlements.

We feel we are standing at a most important juncture in our history. The United States Government has been working to broker a peace agreement between Israel and Syria as well as to keep alive the negotiations between the Palestinians and the Israelis. Many of us are afraid that what might ensue in Palestine is an unjust peace.

We at Sabeel feel we have a Christian responsibility to speak our mind for the sake of a lasting peace that will bring an acceptable justice to the Palestinians and security for all the peoples of our region. We fear that the Palestinian Authority might be forced to accept an unjust peace which will be attractively packaged by the state of Israel and the United States Government. We are, however, sure that an unjust peace will only be temporary and will inevitably plunge our region into greater violence and bloodshed. We will not be silent. We lift our voice prophetically in pointing to the pitfalls of injustice. The following points comprise the different scenarios. We would like to present them clearly with their probable consequences.

The greatest concern: a state of Bantustan

Taking a good look at the Gaza Strip and the West Bank, it is clear that Israel's eye is focused on the West Bank which includes East Jerusalem. The confiscation of Palestinian land, the building and expansion of the settlements have never stopped. Israel continues to insist that the settlements will remain under Israeli rule. If this is done, Israel will maintain its military presence on the West Bank while allowing the Palestinian Authority to have autonomous rule over its own people. The areas under Palestinian rule will be called Palestine. They will have the semblance of a state but will exist under the suzerainty of Israel and will not enjoy genuine sovereignty. What we are witnessing, therefore, is a Bantustan-type state, home rule, just like what was proposed by the former apartheid government of South Africa to its black citizens. From all indications, this is the picture which is emerging on the ground.

If pressured, Israel may even concede the Gaza Strip, where it currently has only 6,100 settlers and controls approximately 40% of the land and one third of the water. It might withdraw totally from the Gaza Strip, which now has a damaged aquifer and a serious lack of usable water, and allow the Palestinians to have their sovereign state there. That area will be small and contained in one corner of Palestine and, from Israel's perspective, will, presumably, not pose any serious threat to Israel. On the West Bank, however, the Palestinians will only be given autonomous rule, a homeland, in the guise of a state yet void of actual sovereignty. This we believe is an unnatural, unhealthy, and unjust scenario and will only lead to a bloodier conflict. History teaches us that oppressed nations will not give up their struggle for freedom and independence. Under this scenario, Israel will not achieve the security it seeks because the forced and unjust peace settlement cannot be permanent. Sabeel rejects outright this peace formula or any variation of it and warns that its imposition will be ultimately catastrophic for both peoples.

The genuine hope: two sovereign and fully democratic states

This scenario envisages the total withdrawal of Israel from all the occupied territories including East Jerusalem according to United Nations resolutions 242 and 338. The Palestinians will establish their sovereign state on the whole of the 23% of the land of Palestine. One way to redeem the settlements is to make them the new towns for the returning Palestinian refugees. This can constitute a part of Israel's reparations to the Palestinians. Israel must compensate the owners from whom the land was confiscated. The Jewish settlers who choose to remain in Palestine can become Palestinian citizens and live under Palestinian sovereignty.

As to Jerusalem, it will have to be shared. The city must remain open to all. A peace treaty will be drawn up and the two countries will become inter-dependent economically and will help each other develop their resources for the well being of both their peoples.

This is the formula which the Palestinians have been hoping and working for. Indeed, it is not the ideal solution, but it carries within it an acceptable justice which most Palestinians are willing to live with for the sake of peace and prosperity. Furthermore, as this scenario agrees with United Nations resolutions since 1967, it will ensure the support of the international community of nations. This formula gives the Palestinians a state as sovereign as Israel, rids them of the Israeli occupation, and restores to them the whole of the occupied territories of 1967. Indeed, a state within the West Bank and Gaza, composed of only 23% of Palestine instead of the 43% allotted by the UN in 1947, is already a very significant compromise by the Palestinians. The Palestinians would have to give up their right to most of historic Palestine. Obviously, Israel, with the help of the United States and the international community, will have to compensate the Palestinian people.

The vision for the future
Our vision involves two sovereign states, Palestine and Israel, who will enter into a confederation or even a federation, possibly with other neighboring countries and where Jerusalem becomes the federal capital. Indeed, the ideal and best solution has always been to envisage ultimately a bi-national state in Palestine-Israel where people are free and equal, living under a constitutional democracy that protects and guarantees all their rights, responsibilities, and duties without racism or discrimination. One state for two nations and three religions. (The spring 2002 Resolution of the Arab League meeting in Beirut, offering "normal relations" with Israel in exchange for the settlement sketched above, may finally offer peace with justice.)

Standing for justice
At every turn, the principle of justice must be upheld. Unless justice is rendered and security is achieved, the solution must be rejected because it will not endure. A just solution must include and equal measure of justice and security for both sides to make it viable. Otherwise it will not lead to a permanent peace. This is the basic principle that must be upheld and used as the measure for every one of the above points.

This is where Sabeel takes its stand. We will stand for justice. We can do no other. Justice alone guarantees a peace that will lead to reconciliation and a life of security and prosperity to all the peoples of our land. By standing on the side of justice, we open ourselves to the work of peace; and working for peace makes us children of God. [We affirm finally, Martin Buber's vision (*On Zion*) of a bilateral nation and a tri-religious culture, a forerunner of biblical Zion where "Swords will be beaten into plowshares" (Isaiah 2:3).][i]

"Blessed are the peacemakers for they shall be called children of God." (Matthew 5:9)
[The Jerusalem Sabeel Document, 2000.]

3

Holy War in Israel

"I will send my terror before you and throw all the peoples into confusion" (Exodus 23:27).

A short excursus now on the mother of all battles of Holy passion. Israel's holy war and its glorification of presumed divine Right of Rule, which colors so deeply the Hebrew Scriptures, has been an enduring, Abrahamic-blessing and Cain-curse to the world. But beyond this two-edged sword Israel is also the hope for justice and shalom in the world. Israel's Abrahamic and akedic destiny is to inaugurate justice (righteousness) in the earth thereby establishing peace.

The reader will be shocked to read these lines. After all, as the Sabeel document has rightly claimed, the modern State of Israel visits a terrible injustice onto the world, an exacerbation yielding unending war. Only a blind fool can see this as the foundation for world peace. How can we explain this hidden destiny, so contradictory of *Realpolitik* and how, in earth history, might this blessed hope of Israel among the nations become manifest?

We must first review the actual mixed legacy of the Holy War history of Israel. We will then parse out the false war and the good war heritage which is the ambivalent historical legacy of Israel. The arrogant and presumptive history, a misreading of the Hebrew bible, creates persistent war and conflict. The history faithful to its justice-in-order-to-peace heritage, one authentic to the norm and vision of Hebrew Scripture, redeems the world. We conclude this chapter with concrete proposals for action today. If the chapter succeeds our thesis will be upheld that rightful Holy passion furthers the righteousness, justice and peace of God, muting and opposing the violence of humanly conceived war.

Another part of my thesis on the war on terrorism is that a deficiency in God-concept leads to Israel's belligerence, Christianity's imperialism and Islam's terrorism. Accuracy in God-concept and God-language is a prerequisite to justice and peace. The religion of Abraham is an historical revelation. Yes it has great mythic stories resonant with all world religion's creation and fall stories: the Adam-Gilgamesh human epic, the flood, Diaspora and restoration. But the mists of primeval myths are soon dispelled as Abraham hears and responds to the call of One who will walk with humanity out into world history. One who will mend a sin-strife, war-torn world by virtue of a redemptive way, enters time and space. Primordial static being is displaced by the "I am," "I will be!" The bible story then unfolds as concrete history—creation and incarnation. Humanity is introduced to a new kind of worldly faith. This is not the projected fantasy of the Greek pantheon or the Hindu spirit-cosmos. This is not "the supernatural invaginating the natural" (contemporary guru). It is Abraham, Isaac and Jacob. It is Moses, Amos and Isaiah. It is the transmutation of King David, Prophet Joshua and Priest Aaron into the man—Messiah, Jesus. It becomes the faith of the Sons of the prophets including Mohammed.

The religion of Abraham becomes a war history. A dialectic is set in motion in Abraham's journey of faith/obedience-doubt/disobedience. Temptation is the trigger of a dialog between good and evil. Temptation entails:

- freedom, choice
- command, warning
- salvation, damnation.

"I set before you life and good, death and evil—choose life" (Deuteronomy 30:15).

Just as a transcending mythic war history—Satan, fallen angels, strife in heaven, overlays and interprets concrete world history, so that concrete world history—oppression, exodus, conquest, exile, Diaspora, Shoah and return, underlies and manifests that transcending redemption. The eschatological and empirical war is a striving in the nature and will of God—cooperating with humankind to secure faith and justice—the parameters of kingdom, the foundations of peace. Let us begin by outlining the events of that war history. Alongside the battle episode we will place the correlate justice-event.

As I read the Hebrew scriptures, in a straightforward, simple (non historico-critical) way, I find the tableaus of terror, threat, temptation, all depictions of strife engaging theology and humanity:

THE PREHISTORY

The Garden, the fall, the banishment	Obedience
Cain and Abel	Killing/violence
Noah/The flood	Immorality
The covenant of life	Noachic covenant
The tower of Babel	Apotheosis

THE PATRIARCHAL HISTORY

Abraham (Hagar/Ishmael, Sarai/Isaac)	Marriage/progeny
Sodom/Gomorrah	Hospitality/violation
AKEDAH (Genesis 22)	Sin/sacrifice
Jacob/Esau/Laban	Usurpation
Joseph and His Brothers	Sibling concord and (kidnapping), forgiveness, international justice
Pharaoh's oppression	Holy War, e.g. oppression, Egypt's planned genocide

THE PROPHETIC HISTORY (Moses to Daniel)

Passover	Akedah reenacted (cosmic sacrifice) consecration
Exodus and the calamity of the Sea	"The Egyptians too are my people;" Miriam's victory song muted
Amalekites and Herem (The Ban)	Holocaust and the horror of conquest
Ascendancy in the land	Measured by righteousness
War Code (Deuteronomy 20)	Just War
Joshua and the Conquest	The Divine Call
The Prophets – Samuel	Power and Vox Dei
Saul/David and the Philistines	Belief/trust; sin/confession; murder, adultery
Solomon	Order/Covenant
The Kings of Israel/Prophets	Justice/Faith/Fall {apostasy, idolatry}
The Kings of Judah/Prophets	Justice/Faith/Fall {immorality, injustice}
Ezra/Nehemiah	Cyrus/Messiah – renewed covenant
Daniel	Idolatry, a war theology of empires

The mixed legacy of Israeli Holy War

What shall we make of this Hebraic war saga which becomes, through Abraham, so constitutive of world civilizations? Again we need to take a broad, surface view, one not obsessed with trivia and minutiae. The history just reviewed forces major theological questions. Given the fact that Israel introduces to the world an ethical deity, a God of history, One who seeks righteousness and sanction, even punishes evil, we are forced to questions such as that raised by Mark Juergensmeyer; is there *Terror in the Mind of God?* (Berkeley: University of California Press, 2000). Or is the imputation of war into the divine being more a projection of our own violence-prone human minds?

We need to peel back the layers of centuries of appropriation of the Hebrew bible to our own situations, our own needs. In the pivotal period of world history, the Anglo-American Puritan moment of history where many modern self concepts, manias and illusions were formed, Cotton Mather and the New England Puritans construed their strife against the Native Americans as recapitulated biblical Holy War. Jonathan Edwards, perhaps the greatest mind of the age, considered by many the finest philosopher that America has produced, fell into disregard in the great congregations of New England. Relegated to being a missionary to Indians on the New England frontier he finally was forced into the ultimate come-down for a pastor. He was named president of Princeton University. Just weeks on the job he succumbed to a small pox vaccination he had taken as an example for the citizens of Princeton.

In Mather's September 1, 1689 sermon "Souldiers Counselled and Comforted" he charges the puritan sons to kill the "murderers" and "wolvish persecutors." Mather's congregation is "Israel in the wilderness" facing "Amalek" which deserves "vengeance and total destruction" (Herem). Not only have the Indians killed Christians ("one Israeli or Christian life is worth 100 Arab Muslim lives") they have been ..."displaced and disinherited by divine decision to make way for the new Israel." (Susan Niditch, *War in the Hebrew Bible*, Oxford: Oxford University Press, 1993, p. 3,4).

Just as the European crusaders had been commissioned against the Saracens in the eleventh century, Israeli settlers in Palestine would be justified and inspired in the twentieth:

> ...on February 24, 1994, the night before the celebration of Purim—a holiday marking the deliverance of Jews from extinction at the hand of their oppressors (he had heard a Palestinian shout "*it bah al-yahud:* slaughter the Jews"), Dr. Baruch Goldstein went to the shrine at the Tomb of the Patriarchs in Hebron/*al Khalil*. The shrine is located above the Cave of Machpelah, the site where Abraham, Sarah and Isaac were said to have been entombed 3000 years ago. The Mosque of Ibrahim had stood here since the 7th century. Goldstein pulled out a Galil assault rifle he had hidden in

his coat and fired into the worshiping throng of men and boys kneeling on the floor...he fired 111 shots, killing 30 and injuring scores more before he was overwhelmed by the crowd and pummeled to death" (Mark Juergensmeyer, *Terror in the Mind of God*, Berkeley: University of California Press, 2000, pp. 49,50).

Use and abuse

The appreciation and misappropriation of Israeli Holy War points us to the ambiguous bible tradition itself. As I sit in biblical seminars at the American Academy of Religion, I see an interesting common thread from exegetes of the Hebrew bible, be they Christian or Jew. On any given biblical passage there seems always to be an apparent meaning, then a contradiction. Holy War passages seem paradoxical like that. Moses, the only prophet to see God face to face, prepares the people to enter the Holy land and dispossess it from the indigenous inhabitants. Then he is not allowed to enter. He had broken faith at the waters of Meribah Kadesh in the Desert of Zin. Joshua, a more militant soul, carries on. David, the man after God's own heart, the adulterer-killer-gentle poet-singer, cannot build the temple. "There's blood on his hands."

And the war texts. The *midrashim* on Miriam's dance-song celebrating the drowning of the Egyptians in the Exodus, seems representative: "Do not celebrate," says the Lord, "They too are my people."

Susan Niditch finds in the Hebrew bible a paradoxical celebration/repudiation of Holy War. From the totalistic, nihilistic imperatives of the Ban in the holocaust requirement against the Amalekites, for example, we move to "the Bardic tradition of war" which is more irenic, steeped, almost like Ecclesiastes in wisdom and the somber tragedy of violence. "The ideology of tricksterism," offers ironic cameos where the lust for conquest and defeat are seen as self contradictory. Ultimately, under a more prophetic eye, the harsh violence of expedient war evolves toward a non-participation, where on the verge of exile, Yahweh's Holy War seems aimed at his own people.

This evolving saga of Holy War leaves the Hebrew bible (Tanakh) at the end of the writings with what Jack Miles depicts as "God's silence." The deep yearnings for peace after weariness of centuries of vicious violence, oppression, brutality and refugee bewilderment, now yearns for deliverance, for Messiah-liberation in justice.

It is possible to tease out these two dialectical threads about war in the biblical tradition. The red thread of national self-adulation and justification tendency of the Hebrew bible is found in Israel Finkelstein's new study, *The Bible Unearthed*. The justice, peace, blue thread can be found in various Christian writers including John Howard Yoder in *The Politics of Jesus*.

The war adulation tradition

As one might expect, contemporary biblical-archeological-historical scholarship about biblical Israel is colored by political persuasions. Pro-Palestinian scholars in Scandinavia, even in Israel, stress the political ambitions to glorify the State as coloring biblical scholarship today.

Most Israeli scholars and American Jewish scholars at millennium's turn feel the need to advocate Israel's existence (of course) and her hegemony (dubious) as they read archeology and history. One exception at the turn of the 20th into the 21st century is the work of the archeologists Israel Finkelstein and Neil Silberman in the important book, *The Bible Unearthed* (New York: The Free Press, 2000).

Finkelstein argues that a political agenda is at work not only in the history of artifact interpretation, including archeology, but in the construction, editing and redaction of the biblical texts themselves. The desire to secure and glorify the State by later redactors may be behind biblical moments such as the Exodus, the Abraham Sagas, The Moses narratives, The Conquest, even the early chronicles of Kings—Saul, David, Solomon. There is precious little evidence that any of the events behind this adulation of the Jewish State actually occurred and close textual and archeological research actually shows another story—one more modest and complicated—than the surviving grand narrative.

According to Finkelstein and Silberman the historical core of Israel's witness is found in the seventh century BCE when a prince named Josiah, "the most righteous of all the kings," discovered a scroll of the law while renovating the temple. His reform purified the rampant idolatry and immorality of the people which had reached even into the temple. It also codified for Judah a national epic with its core in what we now recognize as the Book of Deuteronomy. This epic text of vindications, victory and Holy national glorification, was "edited, amended and enlarged in ensuing centuries to become the Hebrew bible" (Phyllis Trible, "God's Ghostwriters," Review of Israel Finkelstein and Neil Asher Silberman in *The Bible Unearthed*, (New York: The Free Press, 2000) in *New York Times Book Review*, February 4, 2001, p. 16, 17).

The two salient sections of this epic are *Torah*—the first five books and the Deuteronomic history: Joshua, Judges, Samuel and Kings. These two grand narratives extol the saga of the ancestors, "The exodus and wanderings in the wilderness...the conquest of Canaan, the rule of the judges, the establishment of a united monarchy, the destruction of the Northern Kingdom (Israel) by the Assyrians, the destruction of the Southern Kingdom (Judah) by the Babylonians and the beginnings of Exile in Babylon" (16).

The authors then contrast this twofold epic with the archeological and literary data which, they feel, tell a different story:

> The Exodus did not happen as described; the violent, swift and total conquest of Canaan never took place; the pictures of judges leading tribes in battle does not fit the data; David and Solomon existed in the tenth century BC "but as little more than hill country chieftains." There was not golden age of a United Kingdom, a magnificent capital and extended empire (16).

The narratives do serve to ground the national epic by joining the Judean patriarch Abraham together with the Israeli Patriarch Jacob. This conjunction of founders unites preceding events and those which would follow: Moses, Joshua, David, Solomon to buttress the nationalistic 7th century Josiahan claim.

What follows was a glorification of Judea and a domination of Israel centered in a repudiation of Omri, ninth century King of Israel (Samaria). When the Persians liberated the refugees in Babylon after 539 BC a people called *Yehudim* established the province of Yehud, justifying and vindicating its existence with the heroic Abrahamic saga.

Phyllis Trible concludes her review with a cautionary note. The book, says Trible, shows how intertwined are the history and legend—"what happened" and the interpretive imagination.

> That understanding leads to a sobering thought. Stories of exodus
> from oppression and conquest of land, stories of triumphal vision
> are eerily contemporary. If history is written for the present, are
> we doomed to repeat the past? (17).

Another approach to the Hebrew bible's perspective on war, quite in contrast to the nation glorification historiography and the *bellic mimesis* found in Constantine, Cromwell and ultimately El Qaeda, is found in the phrase popularized by Chicago's revered Cardinal Joseph Bernardin—The Gift of Peace.

War as the program for justice and peace
The first premise of this war theology is one expounded by the great theologian—a militant pacifist—John Howard Yoder. In his epic *The Politics of Jesus* (Grand Rapids, Michigan: Eerdmans, 1972), Yoder probes major biblical texts in order to fathom the political witness of Jesus. His chapter on the Hebrew bible is entitled "God will Fight For Us."

In this important passage Yoder goes to the heart of the Hebrew bible's view of war. Reminding us that Jesus irenic commitment is grounded in synagogue life, Hebrew Scripture and the devotion of Second Temple Judaism focused on Shema and Decalogue, he shows the central thrust of the religion of God—the father of the Lord Jesus Christ—the God of Abraham, Isaac and Jacob—to be one of the minimization of war. The thesis is stark: God seeks to protect and save his people without their action. He wills to save them from their enemies and themselves.

He can only do that with their free and faithful obedience. Peace theology is rooted in the hermeneutics of the Exodus. God knows the oppression; He will arise in mighty deliverance. He will strike and afflict the oppressing powers. He will vanquish the enemy. He will show the way out. He will restore Shalom. He will do this with the silent trust, the righteous faithfulness, the saving, non-violent suffering of his people. Did the Hebrews on the scene believe this? Probably not. But their chroniclers with a longer view confessed with faithful hearts across the ages: "He led us all the way..."

Yoder cites the *textus classicus*:

...Fear not, stand firm,
 and see the salvation of the Lord,
 which he will work for your today;
 For the Egyptians whom you see today,
 you shall never see again.
 The Lord will fight for you,
 And you have only to be still (Exodus 14:13).

Well aware that since Auschwitz Jews can never again believe such promises, the strange words point to a peculiar warrior-God. Human operation, even cooperation, is uncalled for. If oppression is authentic and the oppressed are innocent (e.g., not as in the Hebrew exile in Babylon) God, in the force of his justice and care, will remedy the wrong. The people are called only to covenant fidelity—trust and obey.

In the first war on the Amalekites the theocentricity of war and the correlative human passivity is amplified. It is Moses and Joshua who declare war, not YAHWEH. Like Dr. Goldstein at Hebron, humiliation and frustration became too much to bear. So they took justice in their own hands. In Commander-in-Chief George W. Bush's words, "We must bring bin Laden to justice, dead or alive." Now, even beyond Abraham Lincoln, "The judgments of the Lord are not just and right altogether" (Second Inaugural), judgments (military tribunals) are ours. We will deliver.

Exodus 17 symbolizes the shift back to YAHWEH's authority and execution with Moses raising again "The Rod of God" brought down after he wearied of waiting for God's time and decided to "take matters into his own hand." "Praise the Lord and pass the ammunition" war theology took over.

On Reformation Day, 2001, I prefaced the benediction with these words: "Martin Luther trembled at the thought of Muslim Prince Suleiman I massing at the gates of Vienna. A holy warrior indeed, he sought to inspire Europe's princes to the frontier. Yet he knew the only weapon strong enough to defeat the Saracen's was the simple faith and goodness of the village people, devout in prayer and good works in their homes and shops throughout Germany. Slowly, waiting, Suleiman turned back and Europe was spared."

Sermon: The Last Castle
Preached October 31, 2001 Chapel of the Unnamed Faithful
Garrett Seminary, Evanston, Illinois.

THE LAST CASTLE:
HIS FAITH = OUR RIGHTEOUSNESS
The Sea of Faith
Was once, too, at the full, and round earth's shore
Lay like the folds of a bright girdle furl'd.
But now I only hear
Its melancholy, long, withdrawing roar,
Retreating, to the breath
Of the night-wind, down the vast edges drear
And naked shingles of the world.

Matthew Arnold's words in the poem *Dover Beach* are strangely current. 2500, 2000, then 500 years ago, three others heard the ocean's same howling desolation: Habakkuk the Prophet, Paul the Apostle and Martin Luther the Reformer. Reverse the reel. Caught in the hurricane of the modern crises of church and society, as Suleiman the Magnificent massed with his camels, artillery and 600,000 troops at The Gates of Vienna, Luther prayed to be delivered from the fury of the Turk and the rod of divine wrath on himself and his people. As he trembled with terror like Christians today in Pakistan, he was led to the Apostle Paul.

At the most momentous and tumultuous event of spiritual history, the appearance of Jesus as Christ on Earth, just as the world's cosmopolitan power — mighty Rome — marshaled against Judaic rebellion in Palestine, the Apostle had heard the sea roar and the creation groan (Romans 8). To fathom this *kairos* moment he was drawn to Habakkuk. Habakkuk, in turn, had lived during the deepest crux of Hebrew history: The Exile.

Our text is 1:4 and 2:4 of Habakkuk. To paraphrase the words of the prophet to apply to our present situation:

El-Lah (My Lord)…
"Why do you make me watch such terrible injustice? Why do you allow violence, lawlessness, cruelty, terrorism? They scoff at the laws — criminals control the streets."

The Lord responds:
Khalil, (my friend)…
"The insolent and unjust do not belong to me. Only those whom I find righteous in faith."

Habakkuk complained to God that Judah was corrupted by internal injustice and external oppression. The Lord agreed and sent Babylonian terrorists in Holy War punishment of his own people. Habakkuk increased the volume. "El-Lah, but Lord—the Iraqis are even worse!" Khalil, my friend, "I'll take care of them later."

Habakkuk's lament is much like that of Berthold Brecht in the *Three Penny Opera*:

> For what does man live by?
> By hourly torturing, fleecing, attacking, strangling and devouring
> Only by this does man live, that he can so completely
> Forget that he is a man
> My friends make no bones about it; man lives by nothing but his enemies.

Brecht knew that humans either live by violation and violence, or by faith. It was up there on some crude throne—some toilet—that Luther first noticed the words "The just shall live by faith"…words that would change the world.

Lectionary Gospel today finds another man perched up in a tree. That great sycamore still stands today, near Jericho, a few miles out of Jerusalem, down toward the wilderness and the Dead Sea. I climbed it 20 years ago. I hope today that it has not been mowed down by Israeli pilots in American gunship helicopters. It was by that tree that the Rabbi paused as the crowd pressed in. He looked up and shouted with delight—"come down Zaccheus, tonight I will come to your house." While the piety patrol grumbled, Zach cried out: "Rabbi, Elah—My Lord, I give half my estate to the poor." Unlike that young lawyer who asked, "What more must I do?" Zach knew his Torah—the 7th command in Ezekiel 18's Decalogue you recall is, "helping the poor." And he continues, "what I have wrongfully extorted (C/8) by false witness (C/9) I restore fourfold."

In Rabbinic Midrash, Habakkuk 2:4 is like Amos 5:4, the simplest two word summary of the 613-faceted way of Torah. The Zaccheus text is a great gospel text to juxtapose with Habakkuk—it's about the same thing—"the just shall live by faith."

A Decalogic awakening—the delicate equipoise of faith generating obedient life—righteousness in faith.

Up in that tree a twisted soul was grasped by that righteousness through faith. It came in the eyes, the invitation, the grace, the justice, the forgiveness, the companionship of the Master. "Rabbi! My Lord, if I have wronged…" Khalil, my friend, "set another place at the table, tonight I will dine with you." Behold, I stand at the door and knock—if anyone opens the home of his life to me, I will come in and sup with him…" (Emmaeus

again—word, awareness, redirection, the meal at dusk...and burning hearts)
This very hour, Jesus cried, "salvation has dawned on this son of Abraham."
The gift of the Reformation to us and to world history is this salvation—it is
regeneration, liberation, forgiveness, constitution.

Our text revolves around three Hebrew words: Zaddik, Emmuna,
L'hayim—righteousness, faith, life. This is the compound of
salvation—the biblical shalom. In healthful and good progression,
forgiveness leads to faith which leads to freedom which is fulfilled in
sacrificial service. Distorted and contorted freedom leads to indulgence,
exploitation and violence. Reformation becomes deformation.

In wholesome reformation process or what Tillich calls Protestant
spirit, personal faith shapes public life. The continuum goes like this:

Lively personal salvation yields
strenuous conscience which yields
ambiguous freedom.

Reformation is personal and public—it has external and internal meaning.
As European officials sought to persuade Luther to quit reform and oppose
the Muslims, Brother Martin was threatened by an external and an internal
Holy War—the Turks were attacking from without; God was attacking the
Church and his own soul from within, for the terrible failure of faith.
Anfechtung, the accusation of God, was in both assaults.

Consider first the external historical fruits of The Reformation. The
nexus of animated faith proceeds to public manifestations such as:

- right and human rights
- democracy
- industry and enterprise
- the Protestant ethic

The Protestant or Reformed impulse is an ambiguous energy.

In modern life the Protestant Ethic has fashioned processes like
economic free enterprise and global economy, political freedom and human
rights (especially private and formal rights like freedom of religion,
conscience, expression, etc.). It yields philosophical liberalism.
Enlightenment and evangelical awakening are uneasy bedfellows in this
house of Reform.

Though it started earlier, we attribute the rise of nation states to the
Protestant revolution. The celebration of particular peoples is a blessed
release from the oppression of great empires of the past. But, this mood has
also given the modern world the audacity to carve up, dismantle and rename
states. Let's make this Iraq, here Syria; here South Korea, here Israel.

Designating and then not building states has injected turmoil, perhaps interminable conflict, into the modern world.

The ambiguities of global economy also express divine and demonic energies. The world is blest when all peoples on earth can participate in free markets. But, the residue of unbridled greed, vicious competition, demeaning exploitation and environmental degradation disgraces the world and takes us to the verge of calamity as we witness the unconscionable polarity of rich and poor.

Democracy and human rights dignify persons, yet freedom sullies into self-aggrandizement and a "do your own thing" ethic. In the present global crisis, I believe America is falling under the judgment of God along with the brutal terrorists. With Luther we probably find the language of a "weaponizing God:" a fortress, shield, bastion, stronghold. It sounds like God is a Panzer tank. This is treacherous speech, unless God contends not only with our enemies—but also with us. We have visited danger on the world by our rapid exhaustion of global fossil fuels in our demand for cheap energy. We have injected the nuclear threat into world history along with the million innocents we destroyed in Japanese cities. We have despoiled the environment. We have contributed to the global drug culture and its corruption.

With France, Czechoslovakia and China we fill the world with guns and land mines. Along with Russia, we have fueled the threat of biological war by our stockpiles of Anthrax spores and by conspiring in the Cold War. From the first moment when we infected Indian blankets with smallpox we have been biological terrorists.

Reformation freedom is terrible when it is disjoined from service, humility, repentance, responsibility and social justice. This is why the great Protestant and Catholic Reformers, Luther and Erasmus, agreed that perfect freedom was servitude. You remember Luther's words from *Feste Wartburg*: "The Christian is the perfectly free lord of all subject to none. The Christian is the perfectly duty-bound servant of all—subject to all."

All of these abuses of Gospel faith and freedom will continue to ravage the world unless...

> that is Zaccheus comes down from the tree,
> rich and resplendent
> now repentant and receptive
> to become restored and responsible.
> Now he is ready in new-found salvation and freedom to serve
>   messianic justice and redemption
> Ready to sup with this inviting Savior and Lord
> This One who sees and knows not only who we are but who we
>   could be

One who in grace transposes us from here to there.

This leads us to the internal gift of the Reformation. It is the transformation of person's lives, of my life and yours, that is the enduring grace of the Reformation. The encouragement in the personal walk with God in faith. Bach's Feste Burg cantata puts it this way in the powerful bass aria: "He rose triumphant over Satan's hoarde; don't give him your life, it belongs to Jesus." Reformation and All Souls days always flood my soul with gladness and thanksgiving. I always look forward to preaching and celebrating the Lord's Supper on this day. We are especially honored to worship today with my fellow clergy and congregants from First Presbyterian, Evanston. First Presbyterian always has a sizable community at Garrett—faculty, students, staff, Northwestern colleagues—which we trust will grow in the future.

On this day the Vaux family also here remembers with gratitude our parents—Methodists from Indiana, Reformed from Pennsylvania; our grandparents and relatives: Somerset Non-Conformists, English Baptists, Puritans, Scandinavian Lutherans, Ulster Calvinists, French Huguenots, German Reformed—we even have an incognito Swiss Jew—Rosenberg by name; and our Anglican, French Reformed, German Lutheran and Methodist teachers and colleagues. Your vibrant reformation witness has made us who we are and for that we thank God!

The lasting power of the Reformation is changed lives. It is the story of redemption that still changes the world. Luther's story is ours: As he studied Romans and pondered Augustine's confession, he wrote in the preface:

> ...Night and day I pondered until I saw the connection between the justice of God and the statement "The just shall live by his faith."
> ...I longed to know if I could love and be loved by the just God. Then I grasped that the justice of God is that righteousness by which through grace and sheer mercy God justifies us through faith. Thereupon I felt myself to be reborn and to have gone through open doors into paradise.
> If you have a true faith that Christ is your Savior, then at once you have a gracious God, for faith leads you in and opens up God's heart and will; that you should see pure grace and overflowing love.

The outer threat and inner threat were resolved in Ein Feste Burg, *The Last Castle*. Habakkuk, Paul and Luther rightly saw that we had entered earth's final battle. We were now fortified for life's final assault and attack. The first commentary deciphered at Qumran was Habakkuk's (IQ Hab).

This important text introduces both the figure "The teacher of righteousness" and "The Wicked Priest." This writer rightly saw that in these end times we face the consummate eschatological and ethical culmination of world history. Redford's brilliant corpus from *The Horse Whisperer* to *The Last Castle* suggests this ultimate contention—the final castle. There, only as criminals are forgiven and ennobled, restored and emboldened can they defend or contend the kingdom. Such a castle is unassailable and its Akedic knights are irresistible. Any other castle is penetrable. It is as vulnerable as Shakespeare's sad story of the death of kings in Richard II:

> ...It is as if this flesh which walls about our life were, brass
> impregnable and humor'ed thus, comes at the last and with a little
> pin bores through his castle wall and...FAREWELL KING!

But here in Christ's Stronghold, in Feste Burg—in Zion, nothing or no one or no power, can fell us, even death—for one little word—*ein Wortlein* shall fell him. This word—the name of Jesus.

"*Toute le Grace*," sighs the dying priest, in Georges Bernanos and Robert Bresson's *Cure a la Campagne*: All is Grace. Grace is all in all...All is in Christ, in no one or nowhere else...The Reformers sing it—Sola Gratia, Sola Christe, Sola Fidei, Sola Scriptura, and we resound.

Matthew Arnold concludes:

> Ah, love, let us be true
> To one another! For the world, which seems
> To lie before us like a land of dreams,
> So various, so beautiful, so new,
> Hath really neither joy, nor love, nor light,
> Nor certitude, nor peace, nor help for pain;
> And we are here as on a darkling plain
> Swept with confused alarms of struggle and flight,
> Where ignorant armies clash by night.

Yes, he's right, unless that solitary word of Habakkuk is true, "justified by his faith—we live." As the family of grace—communio sanctorum—the congregation of faithful, let us now gather at Christ's table.

Benediction: Luther's prayer was answered. As faith came to life in the highways and houses, in the shops and schools, Suleiman turned back and returned to Constantinople. The enemy within and the enemy without were quelled. Go then into the world in peace—have courage—hold fast to what is good—return no one evil for evil. Support the weak, help the suffering and the God of Peace be with you. Amen.

Waiting on the Lord, discerning His will, examining one's own deeds, pleading for mercy, seeking the peace of the city, such is the central theme in Hebrew war ethics. So much so that even the words of Jesus "love your enemies, pray for those who persecute you" (Matthew 5) and Paul's "If you enemy is hungry, feed him." (Romans 12) are not foreign to the Hebrew testimony.

> ...If Israel would believe and obey, the occupants of the land would be driven out little by little (Exodus 23:29ff) by "the angel" (23:23) or "the terror" (v. 27) or the "hornets" (v. 28) of God (Yoder, p. 81).

The point of this war teaching is God-reliance. C-1 is at stake. Those who trust in national security, power or wealth, those whose ultimate loyalty is to land, language, whose strength is in tanks, chariots and horses, believe, live and act in misdevotion and misdirection. They are a terror to others and a threat to the world.

But self-deception is formidable and national delusion is even more impressive. In the American Civil War both Union and Confederacy thought that their cause was righteous. How is the rightness of cause to be assessed? The test again is the moral tableau of Decalogue in Hebrew conscience or fruit of spirit in Christian conscience. If faith, confession, devotion, honor, piety, love and respect issue forth, the cause is just. If apostasy, idolatry, blasphemy, impiety, disrespect, murder, adultery, stealing, lying and coveting ensue, the cause is unjust.

Testing the spirits, "By their fruits you shall know them" becomes the criterion of discernment. Human action in the world either glorifies God and graces humanity or eclipses God and destroys humanity.

> ...I have set before you life, good and death evil.
> Choose life.
> (Deuteronomy 30:15)

Primal and Persistent Temptation

To believe and to live, in Yoder's reading of Israel's faith and ethics, means to trust categorically, even at the threat of life ("with all one's soul"), that God would honor His word and covenant. This meant that the people would be sustained, the nation not lost and the divine name perpetuated (*Politics of Jesus*, p. 82). The second theme corresponds to the second command. Israel is cautioned against forming alliances in defiance of God and anger over enemies. Alliances form as impulses of self-glory, honor, money and power displace the values of God and good which are the only values worth fighting for. The primal sin of idolatry is the sin of false alliance. The tower of Babel is the constitutive myth where the united races of humanity raise their skyscraper to the gates of heaven in defiance of the counsel of heaven ("Let us make man in our image, in our likeness." Genesis 1:26)

Today (New Year's day, 2002) documents make clear that El Qaeda sought alliance with Iran in an anti-American/Israel Jihad. India and Pakistan amass forces at the border both seeking to firm up alliances especially as Pakistan shifts its forces from the Afghanistan border where it has helped search out al Qaeda forces in its alliance with the U.S. against Taliban. Meanwhile the U.S. seeks to juggle its delicate alliances in the Israeli/Palestinian strife, the India/Pakistan dispute, the Islamic, Orthodox, Catholic disputes in The Balkans, Chechnya, Indonesia, the Philippines and elsewhere.

Prophetic utterance conveys Yahweh's Word and Way as Judah dances with Damascus against Israel:

> Because you relied on the King of Syria,
> And did not rely on the Lord your God,
> The army of the King of Syria has escaped you.
> …you will not need to fight in this battle;
> Take your position, stand still,
> And see the victory of Jahweh on your behalf,
> O Judah and Jerusalem
> Fear not, and be not dismayed;
> Tomorrow go out against them,
> And Jahweh will be with you.
> (II Chronicles 20)

What the prophet calls for is not America's "go it alone" policy advocated by William Safire and some in the Bush administration, who say that we should go into Baghdad and depose Saddam Hussein as Phase II of the war on terrorism, even if we must do this without a single ally in the world. The resistance to alliance is sublimated to rightful singular alliance with the God of history.

When this prophetic claim is viewed against the Finkelstein/Silberman thesis of national exoneration and exultation the *gravitas* of biblical Judaism becomes clear. We should not declare and wage war on our own. Only in extreme circumstances, where the very way of God is at stake, should we resort to violence. Reasons of economics, land-acquisition, cold-war retaliation, revenge and vainglory do not sufficiently authorize either defensive or offensive action. In light of this view of Hebrew scripture the war on terrorism should proceed with caution on its programs of internal security ("*Heimat*") and external assault. When the culprits of El Qaeda are brought to justice, in Afghanistan, Pakistan, Saudi Arabia, Egypt, Europe and America, we should rebuild Afghanistan and   forcefully revise our biased policy and provide two viable and secure nations in Palestine and Israel. Then we could work diplomatically for justice and peace armed with the full blessing of mercy and restoration.

> Not by might nor by power,
> but by my Spirit, says Jahweh of Hosts.
> (Zechariah 4:6)

The holy war legacy of biblical and contemporary Israel offers instruction to the war-prone nations of the world today. Indeed as the great sculpture at the United Nations portrays we seek a world where all nations shall proceed to Zion, there to beat their swords into plowshares, their spears into pruning hooks and in the desert the flowers will blossom.
The legacy of this biblical tradition of justice-grounded peace is Shalom. As J. Pederson noted in his *Israel: Its Life and Culture*, v. II (London's Oxford University Press, 1926, pp. 263, 264):

> In olden time peace is not in itself the opposite of war. There are friends and there are enemies; peace (shalom) consists in complete harmony between friends and (magnanimous) victory in the war against enemies, for in that consists the full development of the soul.

A formidable assault on and rejection of evil and injustice is essential to Holy passion, the fight of God, the war of the Lamb and human social and political policy. More critical by far is the establishment of peace in all its preventive and interventive power. The legacy of biblical Israel will always be the grounding paradigm of this contention.

4
The 20th-century wars against fascism and communism

The focal projection of "evil enemy" in the 20th century for America and most of the world has been the war against fascism and communism. If we ground war ideology in the ethics derived from our foundation in biblical Israel, these systems are twin idolatries, poised in the nationalistic and socialistic poles of the political spectrum. Heresies, these are the exaggerated idols of the "goods" of freedom and equality. The great wars in Europe and Asia in the first half of the century and the more episodic and controversial wars—Korea, Vietnam, the Cold War confrontations in Eastern Europe, Africa, Asia and South America—in the second half, form a complicated ethos which contributes to our thesis.

In the waning decades of the 20th century, the moral controversy centers at root on two values: the *libertas* and *communitas* of responsibility. The legacy of Adam Smith and Karl Marx is manifest in the great value clash of the 20th century. Though China and to a lesser degree Europe fashion socialistic states responsive to the values of communal solidarity, unity and justice, North America, Britain, Israel and Japan fashion nations grounded in Lockean rights and freedoms. At century's close, freedom seems to have prevailed. The Soviet Empire has collapsed, China rushes toward capitalism, only the Muslim world resists infectious liberty. The war on terrorism rises in part out of the moral agonies of this fundamental clash of values. In the first half-century the issue of good and evil was more clear-cut. So much so that General Eisenhower refused to honor the ancient war rule of according dignity to comrades in arms by allowing an official visit to a German general:

> For me, World War II was far too personal a thing to entertain such feelings. Daily as it progressed there grew within me the conviction that, as never before...the forces that stood for human good and men's rights were...confronted by a completely evil conspiracy with which no compromise could be tolerated (quoted

in Michael Walzer, *Just and Unjust Wars*, New York: Basic Books, 1977, p. 37).

Though good and evil seem here so dramatically distinct the reality is more blurred. Harsh settlement of World War I (Treaty of Versailles) creates the condition for World War II. The Communist Revolution early in the century provokes a nationalistic reaction.

The century will refine just war ethics and human rights conventions. It will also create an age of unprecedented cruelty and violence. The age will prove a *Kairos* time witnessing fullness of hope and despair.

Within the purview of metaphysics, metaethics and metahistory—the theology of warfare—the twentieth century is a crossroads where both destructive propensities and peaceful possibilities reach a critical point. The century finds humanity come of age. Science, technology, communications, business and politics weave the world into a global village where all will live and die at the mercy or violence of all others.

The century is the penultimate age. As a wise adage puts it, "this next war will be fought with nukes and the next with sticks and stones." In fact, at century's conclusion, we almost see the simultaneity of stones and lasers in Afghanistan and Palestine. Actually we have entered enough into the future to see that the next war will be fought with terror: germs and boxcutters, Sarin gas and computer viruses. This proves that as the global web of independence and intervulnerability, freedom, choice and responsibility intensifies salvation and damnation hover near—ultimate temptation.

Twentieth-century wars precede our awesome yet agonizing new millennial age. These wars span the mustard gas trenches of World War I strewn with asphyxiated bodies in the first decades of the century through the Enola Gay unleashing her chain reaction bombs over Hiroshima at mid-century, to 500 ton Big Bertha's bombing caves in Afghanistan at century's turn. It begins with Teddy Roosevelt's Rough Rider cavalry charge in Cuba and ends with machete-armed Tutsi and Hutu chopping away in Rwanda. The Communist Revolution in 1917 and end of century liberty revolutions when 80 percent of the world's nations move towards freedom and democracy bookend the awful and inspiring century.

It was the most destructive century of human history. Hundreds of millions of lives were cut short in war, starvation, disease and genocide. We learned that one of every two Jews born since Jesus' day had been killed. What were the wars about? Did they defend and extend freedom? Were they about military power and extending political hegemony? Was the "Godway" in the world extended or diminished?

Overview of a century of war

To answer these questions let us survey the war history of the twentieth century. Luciano Garibaldi [Century of War (New York: Friedman, Fairfax Co., 2001) lists the wars:

- The Anglo-Boer War
- The Boxer Rebellion
- The Russo-Japanese War
- The Italo-Turkish War
- The Balkan War
- World War I
- The Russo-Polish War
- The Italo-Ethiopian War
- The Spanish Civil War
- The Sino-Japanese War
- World War II
- The Indochina War
- The Arab-Israeli Wars
- The Korean War
- The Algerian War
- The Vietnam War
- The Afghanistan War
- The Falklands War
- The Gulf War
- The War at the Horn of Africa
- The Balkan War II

World War I

Pope Benedict XV called World War I "The useless slaughter;" the French called it *la voie sacrée* (the sacred way). For the first time chemical warfare is employed. At Ypres the French troops saw a heart-rending specter as a green-yellow cloud floated toward them with the German army following wearing gas masks. At Verdun we have the first instances of massive indiscriminate bombing of civilians. Every family in France and Germany, most in Britain and many in America were torn by grief and heartbreak.

In the confusing dying days of World War I, Lenin and Trotsky, fueled by Marx and the furious inhumanity of early industrial Europe and the first world war in Europe, achieved a *putsch* in Russia where the Czar, like the first Kaiser and the *dritte Reich* Kaiser to follow would fall and a new social order ensue. Though a minor skirmish against the somber backdrop of the first war, the social changes let loose by the Communist Revolution would deeply influence the century to follow.

The Italian and Ethiopian War (1935-1936), the Spanish Civil War (1936-1939) and the Chinese-Japanese War (1937-1938) not only exaggerated the brutality of World War I but set the stage for the first and hopefully the last global conflagration, World War II. Pablo Picasso's harshly cubist mural *Guernica* howls with anguish of land and animals, youth, elders and children—agonizing preludes to the "Great" and Studs Terkel's "Good War."

In his World War II essay "Midway" (*Carnage and Culture*, New York: Doubleday, 2001, p. 7) historian Victor Davis Hanson continues to develop his thesis that Western ideas and practices of war serve the underlying values of freedom (faith, speech, movement, etc.) and democracy which values in turn invigorate the fighting spirit. In his chapter on "Midway" he focuses the values and virtues of individuality, courage and relentless fighting by headlining a quote from Hippocrates, *Airs, Waters, Places* (16, 23):

> ...[where] men's souls are enslaved they refuse to run risks readily and recklessly to increase the power of somebody else. But independent people, taking risks on their own behalf and not on behalf of others, are willing and eager to enter into danger for they themselves enjoy the prize of victory...

In the greatest aircraft carrier battle in the history of naval warfare (June 4-8, 1942), in a surprise attack as devastating as Pearl Harbor, "in less than twelve hours" the heart of the Japanese fleet of carriers—the Akagi, Kaga, Hiryu and Soryu—were set afire and "the course of World War II in the Pacific radically altered" (Hanson, 335).

My Princeton Seminary classmate Blaine Libby, later naval commander on the carrier Midway, often related the proud history of the battle. Hanson writes:

> ...The Americans would lose dozens of carriers, battleships and cruisers...to brave and brilliant Japanese sailors and pilots... On Guadalcanal (see Terrence Malick's film *The Thin Red Line*) Tarawa, Iwo Jima, Okinawa...thousands of Americans would be slaughtered by well-planned and organized Japanese assaults. Yet the astounding fact remains: in less than two years, after being surprised and caught in a state of virtual unpreparedness, the United States not only defeated an enormous and seasoned Japanese military but destroyed (only to rebuild) the Japanese nation itself...

How?...

- "a long tradition of reliance on individual initiative"
- creating [a culture] of "brilliant and highly idiosyncratic leaders"
- "...who relied on their own initiative and autonomy to wage war"
- when persons act as "individuals...they prize their freedom" (385ff.)

Hanson, Keegan and the war historians have it half-right. There was, in World War II especially, an enormous love of freedom. Yet this self-sacrificing ardor for liberty was undergirded by a love for their fellow man, especially the military buddies, by holy passion for the folk back home and for the peoples whose lands had been oppressed, whose ancestors were also their ancestors (e.g. Germany, England). There was also a holy passion of lethal anger at those like Hitler who set out to destroy not only our people but their own. Finally there was a confidence that divine providence and grace "righteoused" their action. The pivotal wars of the twentieth century were ultimately theological wars—wars to protect and sustain a divinely condoned way of truth and life—belief, confession, sanctity, life-affirmation, equality, liberty, love and justice. They were therefore wars against a demonic heresy: apostate idolatry, blasphemy, desecration, destruction, harm, injustice, oppression.

The wars against fascism then communism resisted collectivism and false lordship and oppression over humanity. While at war's end the victor violations of justice burgeon and pride compounds, leading to transgressions such as the civilian bombings of German and Japanese cities, the major endeavor of the wars was a search for holy passion-for righteousness. In the East and West tribunals sought to draw moral lessons and precedents from the wars. Military officers and political leaders were accused of crimes against peace, war crimes and crimes against humanity. Assuming that wrong had been done against the world in the initial aggression and in the underlying causes (e.g. Shoah) new punishments were required and new rules were laid down and resolves (concords and treaties) were formulated.

Even today (January 2002) as most of Europe adopts the Euro as its official currency the world hopes that this at last will insure peace so that the entire world will not suffer again the loss of life, the diversions of resources, the disruption of life caused by the great wars in Europe. Yet, even now, the dust still stirs at ground zero at the base of the World Trade Center and shots are heard from the labyrinth of caves near Kandahar, Afghanistan.

What were the lessons learned—the goods confirmed and the evils further attested in the Second World War? The war ended the lives of at least 50 million people, injuring another hundred million. The Soviet Union lost 15 million persons, soldiers and civilians. Her commitment to subsequent security efforts, cold war nuclear armament and late twentieth century peace leadership are well understood. Her advocacy against the US, of nuclear treaties, peace impulses in the aftermath of Afghanistan and balanced support/critique of Israel and Palestine are well placed.

Poland lost 20 percent of its population—six million persons. One half of these were Jews—three times the number of German Jews killed. Six million Germans died. Most other participating countries lost one million plus lives, a significant number for small-population peoples. As in the 17th century where wars of religion simply wore people out, this great war would turn the heart of humanity toward institutions of peace, the United Nations, global economy, multi-ethnic and cross-cultural understanding, and the like. Ethics in public life, in medicine, military, law and business would flourish. Religion took a new seriousness as acculturated Western Judaism mutated toward Zionist orthodoxy and vibrant Conservative and Reformed synagogue life. Christianity, though often captive to culture forms and norms, experienced new vitality especially in Roman Catholic, evangelical and holiness traditions. Islam, though static and still defensive, began to recover some of the vitality it had experienced in the early Middle Ages.

War had sharpened in the conscientious sensibilities of humanity the antinomies of good and evil, justice and injustice, revenge and forgiveness, hope and despair, love and hate. The world became much more attuned to its own complicity in evil, to the necessity of preventive and preemptive efforts for peace, for the establishment of justice foundations for long-range *shalom*.

World War II and Beyond

Only months after the death camps in Poland are liberated and the Japanese surrender to MacArthur aboard the battleship Missouri in Tokyo Bay, a tragic aftermath unfolds which will haunt the rest of the century. In the northern mountains of Greece ELAS (communist) guerillas prepare to continue their war against fascist, even democratic government. In Palestine Haganah, the Zionist militia begins stepped-up terrorist sabotage against the mandate government. In the far-east Chinese, Vietnamese and Korean communists begin plans to exploit Japan's vulnerability and the political unrest of war's end. So in the West, Mid-east and Far East seeds of strife are being planted even as martyr's blood still cries to heaven on the Rhine and the Ardennes, on the sands of North Africa, at Iwo Jima and Nagasaki.

Korea

Almost predictably, while General MacArthur supervised Japanese reconstruction from Tokyo, at 4 a.m. on June 25, 1950, when my Princeton Seminary classmate, Syngman Rhee, governed in Seoul, just 25 miles to the south, North Korea began launching long range artillery shells across the 38th parallel. Within hours a full-scale invasion of infantry supported by 150 Soviet-made T 34 tanks began a blitzkrieg that what would conquer Seoul in two days. Immediate alarm rung through Washington and President Harry Truman's office, that of Secretary of State Dean Acheson, that of his special advisor, Presbyterian warrior John Foster Dulles, his chair of the Joint Chief of Staff General Omar Bradley and that of United Nations Secretary-General Trygve Lie of Norway. All marshaled a quick counter-reaction and the first of a new set of wars—wars declared and fought by United Nations mandate—had begun. The UN declared, "...it [UN] will furnish such assistance to the republic of Korea as to be necessary to repel armed attack and restore international peace and security in the area."

Korea, of all Asian nations, presents an intriguing conflict between Hanson's occidental and oriental types—one oriented toward individualistic freedom and the other toward communal conformity. Korea was an anomaly—so deeply shaped by Protestant missionaries, Presbyterian and Methodist—at the dawn of the twentieth century. Japan had been impervious to Christian influence. The witness had thrived somewhat in China until extinguished first by the Boxer rebellion then by Mao Tse Tung's communism. But the Korean peninsula has proven amazingly open to the protestant gospel and ethos. So great was the affinity with American ideals and values that today there will soon be more Korean Presbyterian and Methodist churches in greater Chicago than all other Presbyterian and Methodist congregations.

In his two volume *Origins of the Korean War* (1945-1947) (Princeton: Princeton University Press) Bruce Cummings faults the Protestant churches for abandoning the north along with their church colleagues and fleeing south, forsaking solidarity in the gospel for reasons of political freedom and economic capitalism. Yet theological issues of war became paramount as with the Jesuits in the Philippines and Anglicans in China. Persecution (war because of faith) becomes rampant in the north.

My seminary, Princeton Theological, in its last alumni magazine (Dec. 2001) honors its martyred pastors over the last century. French Protestants under Hitler, Czechs under communism, Latin American missionaries under many oppressive (often US supported) regimes. Then a small footnote—"and some hundreds of Korean martyr pastors." Most of these were church leaders who suffered and died under the intrusion of communism into the peninsula. Yet today Methodist and Presbyterian pastors, laypersons and theologians, form the *avant guard* leadership in the quest for Korean reunification.

Freedom of religion and belief, a derivative of the first commandment, thus becomes crucial in the moral analysis of this war. Of secondary but vital import are the 7-10 commandments which commend justice and condemn economic exploitation and disregard of the poor. The South of Korea like the South of the US in the final Cousins War (1861-1965) has been contemptuous and neglectful of the poor. Commentators have drawn the ideological analogy of the first war with Communism, the war with fascism which proceeded precipitated it and the war on terrorism. Just as America once opposed fascism and communism as an insidious ideology, today we must oppose "fundamentalist political Islam." Claims Newsweek International correspondent Feres Zakari:

> We should set up Islamic academies showing the wider range of values in Islam. We should work for greater freedoms (press, speech, religion) etc. in countries like Saudi Arabia, Egypt, Jordan and the like so that these peoples will not be so oppressed and restricted to the radical thought of the anti-American political Islamic thought. We should attend to the political aspects of globalization not just the economic" (*Newsweek, News Hour with Jim Lehrer*, Thurs. Jan 3 2002).

Truman's crisis speech on the Korean attack sounded apocalyptic, Churchillian "Iron Curtain" rhetoric:

> The attack upon Korea makes it plain beyond a doubt that communism has passed beyond the use of subversion to conquer independent nations and will now use armed invasion and war (Robert J. Dyorchak, *Battle for Korea*, Pennsylvania: Combined Publishers, 2000, p. 11).

The archenemy of Hitler and fascism had already ceded to Stalin and Russia before Potsdam. The foreboding fear of the "godless" communist revolution in 1919, especially in its subversion of capitalist economics and establishment politics in the West, was an undercurrent of political theology even during the Second World War. Fervent anticommunists like Presbyterian, John Foster Dulles, were formulating what eventually would become Ronald Reagan's "Evil Empire" theodicy and George W. Bush's "evil axis" theodicy.

But the Korean War would become the first war, even before Vietnam, that "America would lose" (see Bevin Alexander, *Korea: The First War We Lost* (New York: Hippocrene Books, 2000). In the fury of revenge and patriotic fervor against that invasion of the South by North Korea, America, Syngnam Rhee's South Korea and the token UN coalition invaded the North after the Inchon invasion of September 1950. It failed. Therefore the only course of possible action despite MacArthur's foolhardy counsel to go into China and American anticommunist hawks assent and China and North Korea's misguided ambition to conquer the South, was a partitioned peninsula.

The theology of heroic American liberty and diabolic communist oppression, though deeply flawed, would persist through the third, even fourth quarter of the century. It would sustain a fatal blow in Vietnam.

Vietnam

When a patriot like Senator Bob Kerry, lamed from a wound in the Vietnam war, rises to express remorse or from the other side of the isle when Senator John McCain, a prisoner of war for many years, visits North Vietnam in reconciliation we are aware that deep soul searching about rectitude and guilt is going on. The parade of great films about Vietnam—*The Deer Hunter*, *Coming Home*, *Born in the USA*, *Apocalypse Now*, *Platoon*, *Full Metal Jacket*—are all protest, anti-war documents. Even *Ali* in the year 2001 recalls with approving nostalgia one who said "what have the Viet Cong ever done to hurt me?"

Photos brought a hesitancy early and late: Eddie Adam's Pulitzer Prize winner of South Vietnamese General Nguyen Ngoo Loan blasting the right temple away of a suspected Viet Cong; a Buddhist monk immolating himself in the middle of a busy Saigon street; the shudder of horror when peasant villages are torched at Mai Lai; Larry Lichty's series *Vietnam: the American Experience*.

When America decided to fight in Vietnam in 1965 a national and international consensus esteemed them as defenders of justice and prime freedom fighters in the world. Her sacrifice in WW II and Korea had challenged the tyrannies of fascism and communism. Her noble efforts to defeat racism and poverty in the Civil Rights Movement had all the world singing "We shall overcome." By 1975, when Saigon fell, that same national consensus and international esteem had changed to profound doubt and embarrassment about one's country. As one of the generation of young pastors and theologians schooled in the early 1960's, taking one's post as an evangelist for Gospel salvation and for social justice (with most of my contemporaries), I found myself disenchanted with my country. Though church and society could not stomach our protest from pen and pulpit initially, our disenchantment eventually carried the day. By that time most of us were out of the church and now serving as university professors, or presidents, bioethicists, social workers, foundation directors or like our colleague at Northwestern, Gary Wills, historian—writers, *par excellence*.

The war in Vietnam was a working out of American policies to combat communism formulated after the Korean War, specifically by President Eisenhower and his advisors from 1954-1956. Crises in Laos and South Vietnam in 1960-1961 led President Kennedy, in response to that theology of foreign policy, to lay plans for eventual action in Indochina. Starting with American advisors in 1962, American leaders in the Kennedy and Johnson administrations—the "best and brightest of their generation", as David Halberstam has said—"liberal humanitarian scholars all"—increasingly followed an idealist template of analysis and action which saw the stipulation of freedom as antithetical to the imperatives of communism. The Russian and Chinese bear had to be killed.

With a more noble and just government in South Vietnam, without the Buddhist crisis of 1963, without the uncanny credibility and verve of Ho Chi Minh and the North Vietnamese society, the America-led freedom coalition might have succeeded. But the smile of the Cheshire cat lingered from the French incursion of the preceding decades. Kennedy's intriguing rapprochement with Europe and even Russia, shattered in the Cuban Missile Crisis of 1962, ended with his assassination in 1963. By March of 1965 America was bombing and napalming the North and the Viet Cong strongholds in the South. Firm, resolute and forceful preemptive action against Germany and Japan, Russia, Korea and China, it was thought in retrospect, might have foreshortened those moments of tyrannical curse on humanity. Lyndon Johnson and Richard Nixon, men we know from subsequent research to be very political, compromising and somewhat amoral beings, succumbed to the spiritual and moral equivocation of the American people. Torn between social-justice multiculturalism and evangelical nationalism, they led America and the world into a tragic, but ultimately redemptive, futile war.

In the closing decades of the twentieth century freedom, democracy and capitalism would become one irresistible force in the world. The Soviet Union would collapse by its own weight and by its expenditure into cultural exhaustion trying to compete with the US in the Cold War. Today as a decade of economic debacles cripples Argentina, causing the world to have second thoughts about globalization, as technophilic, yet traditional China plays out its enigmatic global destiny, as the Islamic world struggles with the tension between a zealous, Shariah-grounded political theocracy and a more secular-pluralistic ethos and as Turkey volunteers to succeed Great Britain as second head of the peacemaking force in Afghanistan, the world withdraws, takes pause to get its breath, and recoils in horror as the twin Babel towers of he World Trade Center collapse.

The century to end all centuries, the most violent in human history—one which prompts great philosophers like Richard Leaky (African anthropologist) to say that the world would not survive another such century—a century which thought several times that this present war would be the war to end all wars, now hopes on in realistic yet solemn yearning. It is Epiphany 2002, as I write these reflections. The world celebrates wise men journeying from the East, perhaps from Baghdad and Mogadishu, to Palestinian Bethlehem and that claptrap, quasi-restitution of Solomon's imperial Judea. PLO Chairman Arafat is forbidden by Israel to kneel at the Bethlehem manger on Christmas Eve. Yet the world still yearns for a song of peace across those hills.

"Glory to God in the highest and peace on earth among people of good will."

5

Primitive Christian pacifism to Constantinian power

The best way to protect the homeland is to unleash the military...
President George W. Bush in Asia, Feb. 17, 2002

Raise the war cry, you nations and be shattered!
Listen all you distant lands.
Prepare for battle, and be shattered!
Prepare for battle and be shattered!
Devise your strategy, but it will be thwarted;
Prepare you plan, but it will not stand,
For God is with us.

Every warrior's boot used in battle
and every garment rolled in blood
will be destined for burning,
will be fuel for the fire.
For unto us a child is born...
The government shall be on his shoulders
His name... prince of peace
(Isaiah 8,9)

It is Sunday before Palm Sunday, 2002. Worshippers gather in the Protestant International Church near the US embassy in Islamabad, Pakistan. As they sing the praise hymn, "We are Standing on Holy Ground" two men walked in and threw hand-grenades into the throng. Five persons were killed and 40 seriously wounded. The proclamation of the Gospel itself is now threatened. It's time for Holy war, right? Wrong! Holy War theologians from Augustine to Luther would claim that if we are persecuted even killed for proclaiming the gospel we must respond with Jesus' passive resistance. ...How on earth?

In the moving sequel to his Pulitzer Prize winning *God: A Biography*, Jack Miles explores the strange paradox at the center of the new, now ancient, divine dispensation to the world. *Christ: A Crisis in the Life of God* (New York: Knopf, 2001). At the heart of that paradox is a war that appears impotent, a vulnerability and sacrifice with efficacy, a broken plan which will mend and restore the world. Recapitulating the ancient *AKEDAH* of Abraham, that paradoxical primal faith where "letting go" and "giving over" yield "receiving back" and "going on", Miles looks with vivid literary wonder at the phenomenon of Christ – the anointed king who must die, the warrior who must fall and fail, the defeated One who defeats the one in the world who seems to defeat all.

The panorama of inaugural events into messianic destiny – baptism and temptations – is penetrated by the crazed vision of John the Baptist, "Behold the lamb of God who takes away the sins of the world" (John 1:29-31) and the baptismal voice from heaven, "...This is my beloved son...with you am I well pleased (Mark 1:11) and the temple taunts: "If you are the Son of God..." (Luke 4:1-13).

All are refer to the *akedah*, as do all texts with "lamb of God," "beloved son," and "only begotten son." They recall Abraham's frightening summons: "Take your son...your only son, the one you love dearly". Go to Moriah...sacrifice him there" (Genesis 22:2ff). They also recall the savior/servant Psalm (2:7-9):

> He said to me:
> You are my son;
> This day have I begotten you.
> ...I will make the nations your inheritance.
> You shall break them with rods of iron...

Miles agonizes: "The improbable and appalling conjunction of expiatory lamb and messianic war lord receives its first statement here" (27).

Akedic references are all about war:

- They are about the primal war transpiring between heaven and earth.
- They are about the weight of injustice and wrong that besets the world.
- They are about the contention of the inertia and inequity with the emergence of the holy and the good into reality...
- They are about the sacrifice entailed in the defeat of that very evil.
- They are about temptation endured and conquered which is the bestowal of freedom, and receipt of salvation.
- They are about the commandment to faith and life – the choice between right and wrong – the price which that contest will exact.

- They are about war.

The appearance of Jesus as Christ bestows a new military ethos on the world. The gift of forgiveness ("repent, and be baptized") sets in place and motion a decisive truce which requires laying down our arms.

> ...He is our peace
> Who has broken down the dividing wall of hostility
> He broke it through His cross
> Where he put hostility to death
> (Ephesians 2:14-16)

The temptations: "If you are the Son...?"

> Turn these stones to bread
> All these kingdoms I give you...
> Throw yourself down...

Frame the New Testament lives of Christ (Matthew 4, Luke 4). They inaugurate the initial challenge to his annunciated mission: A warrior dictum:

> I come to release the captives...
> to dispatch good news to the poor
> to proclaim the Jubilee (Luke 4:18-19)

And they are reenacted on the cross:

> If you are the Son...
> ...come down

Bracketing the earth-life of the Christ these events – temptation and the cross – are cast in the *akedic* format [call . test . sacrifice . restoration] and in the logic of temptation [command . choice . cost . consummation]. Yoder notes that the temptations explore three dimensions of *casus belli* – reasons for war (*Politics of Jesus*, p. 32ff):

- Economic desire
- Socio-political ambition
- Blasphemy

The answer of the desert warrior and the crucified one is decalogic:

- Man does not live by bread alone but by every word

- Worship and serve God alone
- Do not tempt the Lord your God

Can the charismatic leader, the anointed deliverer, prevail in Holy war?
Can he

- Reenact the food miracles (Moses) in the desert (Deut. 8:3A)
- Receive the surrender of enemies "handed over" (Jeremiah 27:4 ff)
- Invoke divine invulnerability ("no harm will befall you," Psalm 9)

…all constructs of Israel (Judah's) holy war?

Yet, in enigmatic mystery

"the bread and water" of life hungers and thirsts
the giver of life is "given over" to powers
the one in whom all power in heaven and earth is given (Matthew 28) is
placed at the mercy of the world

With extraordinary insight Miles sketches the total "inversion of values"
which so offended Nietzsche who rather demands

… not contentedness but more power;
not peace but war…
The Antichrist (Q, Miles p. 6).

A new template to assess power and to evaluate war is being proffered. A
holy hesitancy now mutes holy passion. This reserve will contour Holy
war, Crusade and Jihad by interposing another messianic destiny as the
deepest meaning of Abraham's *Hegira*. This then becomes the paradigm of
the derivative quest and conquest that will be the historical concourse of his
threefold progeny: Judaism, Christianity and Islam.

Having set the stage for a surprising and radically new perspective on
holy passion and war my plan in this chapter is to now discuss the thesis of
this study in light of the two central sections of Mile's Christ:

- The Roman *Shoah* and the disarmament of God and
- The price of His pacifism: John is murdered

Shoah
Miles' central contention is that the warrior God of Israel; Holy war (+
Christian crusade and Islamic Jihad) has to be disarmed. God in the Christ,
knew that genocide (*Shoah*) by the Roman empire on His chosen people

was immanent. He resolved to not conspire insurrection against it. With Yasir Arafat (Good Friday, 2002) he "could see one million martyrs marching to Jerusalem". But he left them disappointed. In contrast to the argument of Roman's specialist Bob Jewett (unpublished paper "Chariots of Fire: War in the Bible"), who contends that Jesus sensed that the mounting calamity would destroy and disperse the Jewish people (the Roman wars 66-73 C.E.) and therefore sought to avert it, Miles sees Jesus carrying the "white flag" of surrender. The gospel texts are explanations of God's "scandalous inaction" (p. 109).

> ...The Gospel is scandal (*skandalon*, Greek)
> a stumbling block to the Jews (who seek manifest power)
> and foolishness to the Greeks (who seek wisdom and common sense) (I Corinthians 1).

Citing the philosophy of war history in Daniel (Ch 7) that empires – Greek, Roman and Persian – will rise but God will ultimately deliver his people, Miles verdict is stark: Will god keep his promise to deliver? God didn't and He won't!

The Roman slaughter of Jews in first century Palestine was of near equal magnitude to the twentieth century *Shoah*. By rough estimates, 1 million of 6 million Judaic population in the first century were killed and 6 million of 25 million in the twentieth century.

Concentrated in Palestine (perhaps 2.5 million) with another 3.5 million in proximate Diaspora, first century Jews found their spiritual and secular epicenter in Jerusalem. This faith community fervently believed that the Messiah would physically deliver and restore David's kingdom as Daniel's "son of man" led the god-derived holy war against Rome. As with Albert Schweitzer's Jesus in *The Quest for the Historical Jesus*, they believed that God would act decisively, defeating Rome and establishing their realm (Schweitzer went so far as to assert that Jesus died under this illusion and disappointment sacrificing himself – casting himself on "the wheel of the world"—which rolled on to crush him). Schweitzer concludes with the enigmatic words: "that is his victory and his reign".

But with Christians of all ages we read the war theology of Israel/Judea differently than Schweitzer or Finklestein/Silberman. I take seriously the subtle shift in historical theology from God as warrior-victor in 10th – 8th century Israeli history to God as antagonist/punisher of his now victim people, in the invasions, exile and restoration of the 7th through 2nd centuries BCE. As scripture sees the victories of Assyria and Babylonia as the punitive actions of God it becomes clear that God now holds Israel (and the church and Islam) accountable to Torah faith and justice just as he holds her enemies accountable. In those tragic pre-1967 events in Palestine which

precipitated the current crisis of terrorism, Christian Arabs, Jewish and
Muslim radicals all provoked terror. They all attenuated the peace – then
and now. Miles finds a more profound and radical capitulation in the
historical novel of the Old and now the New Testament. In his reading God
concedes failure, disarms and sets out on a new course.

> ...The God who will no longer reward or punish
> his covenant partners as he once did can no
> longer require of them what he once required.
> Henceforth, it is not their devotion to him but
> their devotion to one another and, even more
> remarkably, to strangers (and enemies) that will
> signal their status as his – to the extent that
> they keep this one commandment
> (John 13:34, Galatians 5:14),
> to that extent the divine warrior will be excused
> from ever again taking up arms
> (p. 115 – brackets my additions).

...rather than establish the kingdom of God by military force, he preaches
military renunciation (p. 115).

In my view and in the argument we are exploring in this book, I
propose that this apparent failure and capitulation of God in Jesus may
actually be the command and victory of God. This plan is as eternal as
Torah, Akedah, and Christ, the transcending design of God for creation.
Still this notion can only be posed as a heart-wrenching question not as
triumphalist confidence.

Abraham Joshua Heschel prefaces his landmark *The Prophets* with a
dedication drawn from Psalm 44 to the martyrs of 1940-1945:

> All this has come upon us,
> Though we have not forgotten thee,
> Or been false to Thy covenant.
> Our heart has not turned back,
> Nor have our steps departed from Thy way
> ...for thy sake we are slain...
> (we are like sheep to be slaughtered)
> Why dost Thou hide Thy face? (From Psalm 44 , my addition)

Heschel's (and the psalmist's) conjunction both deepens and refutes the
disjunction of command faithfulness and suffering that Miles is proposing.
A Christian messianism and war theology is *akedic*. This perspective
contends that when we remain true to God and "in the Way" we will

inevitably suffer as messiah suffers through the history of creation. We cannot expect a Deuteronomic destiny of unending welfare. This leads to a variant theology of war. In this purview the David-like, stone-slinging Palestinians who die may be the real hero's and not the Israeli's sweeping in for the kill in their American-provided gunship helicopters. God arms and vindicates the oppressed not the mighty. Here the peasant Afghan Taliban fighters and not the high tech mega-killers or Osama bin Ladens nor the American precision bombers may ultimately "sway the future" (James Russell Lowell).

> ...He has put down the mighty from their perches and
> lifted up the lowly (Luke 1:52 also Isaiah, Psalms and specifically I
> Samuel 2)

Pacifism
Miles now turns to yet another complex irony involving Jesus and John the Baptist. This is another view transformative of the militant way offered in primitive Christianity. Even as Jesus in irenic military annunciation, proclaims that he comes "to set the prisoner free", his baptismal pastor, John, languishes toward death in Herod's prison. John's continuing incarceration and the doubts raised by his mentor's inaction may have prompted his dispatch to Jesus: "Are you the one to come or shall we look for another?" (Luke 8:18ff).

Following on the heels of Mile's section on the Roman Shoah and the disarmament of God Miles offers an equally provocative theme "the Price of His Pacifism: John is murdered." His argument here is that John had been mislead into a militant messianism literally becoming "captive" with the expectancy literally of being "set at liberty." Now with the fracture of this emancipation there is hesitancy in his dispatch: "...are you the one to come or shall we expect another?"

Now Jesus says

> ...Until John the law and prophets prevailed
> now the Kingdom of God is come,
> ...blessed are those who have faith (p. 119).

Jesus is consigning John to his fate, claims Miles.

Miles asks if John really expected this strong emancipator, who Entebbe-like would sweep in on helicopters to his rescue or did he really see something new when he pointed to Jesus: "...Behold the lamb of God."

I hold to the latter reading. And in view of our thesis this event is sustenance not severance of the prophetic tradition where we must fight for God and good. We are called to wage with Jesus the war for justice and peace and point to two elements of this conjunction of command and conquest in John the Baptist's story. First Jesus' answer back to John is decalogic – it points to "fruit of ministry"—tell John what you have seen and heard:

> …the lame walk, the deaf hear,
> the dead are raised to life and the poor
> hear the good news
> (Luke 8:15ff).

That is our war character. It is a crystal summary of the decalogic/*akedah* or the heart of Abrahamic religion when messiah reigns as *Torah* is accomplished. The godly and humanly "high-way" is made straight in the desert (Isaiah 40). Furthermore John the Baptist's death-provoking preaching at Herod's compound is thoroughly decalogic (rooted in the distillation of *Torah*) as is his instruction to soldiers, debtors and workers (Luke 3:10-14).

In the preaching near Schechem which brought down Herod's ire and ultimately, at Salome's request, his sword on John's head, he commented on Commandments 7 and 8 on adultery and on "…all other evils that Herod had done" (Luke 3:19). We might imagine that the broader context here was something like Jesus' Sermon on the Mount, a week-long midrash/sermon about the Shemah and Decalogue, which was the pivotal authoritative text of faith and life in Jesus' (second temple) time.

Even more specifically decalogic and rigorously faithful to the commands (c. 8-10) to honor the poor and weak (see Ezekiel 18) is the baptist's counsel to multiple queries:

> 7 He said therefore to the multitudes that came out to be baptized by him, "You brood of vipers! Who warned you to flee from the wrath to come? 8 Bear fruits that befit repentance, and do not begin to say to yourselves, 'We have Abraham as our father'; for I tell you, God is able from these stones to raise up children to Abraham. 9 Even now the axe is laid to the root of the trees; every tree therefore that does not bear good fruit is cut down and thrown into the fire."
> 10 And the multitudes asked him, "What then shall we do?" 11 And he answered them, "He who has two coats, let him share with him who has none; and he who has food, let him do likewise." 12 Tax collectors also came to be baptized, and said to him, "Teacher, what shall we do?" 13 And he said to them, "Collect no more than is appointed you." 14 Soldiers also asked him, "And we, what shall we do?" And he said to them, "Rob no one by

violence or by false accusation, and be content with your wages" (Luke 3:7-14).

We may forgive Luke's Hellenism and anti-Semitism because he sees rightly that war for fidelity (faith) and justice is the gist of what the Baptist calls for in confession "repentance" (*metanoia* or decalogic return), receipt of forgiveness, belief and "works" worthy of repentance. This alteration of conviction and emendation of life-style is, in our thesis, the essence of what we must defend and fight for in our life in the world. This faith-life conjunction is the essence of God's way for humans in the world for which he has given his Son to the world and co-suffered with his Abrahamic *Akedic* people.

The history of the early Christians will begin as tribulation and persecution as they live out *akedic*/decalogic existence – "The war of the lamb". This is attested by the Good Shepherd – lamb motif in their catacombs art. The way of this Jesus community comes to prevail in the Roman Empire because of the war of defense and offense. It fights <u>against</u> apostasy, idolatry, immorality and injustice specifically in opposing "Empire worship", blasphemy (denying "Name"), abortion, infanticide, sexual promiscuity including pederasty, extortion and exploitation of the poor. It fights <u>for</u> faith, free-confession, pacifism, chastity, love and provision for the needy. Let us follow these two developments of resistance and redemption in early Christianity.

Persecution
Persecution of the nascent Christian community begins close on the days of Pentecost with the crisis around Stevens' stoning (early 30 CE). It continues the persecution of Roman Christians under Nero (c. 64 CE), the stoning and execution of James, Jesus' brother (62 CE) and the probable martyrdom of Peter and Paul, perhaps in the same year.
What is it about the collective witness that provoked their executions? In thumbnail sketch these primal preachers-martyrs posed a radical exclusivity of belief – "One God" – and a radical ethic, "see how they love one another" (John 13:35, Acts 7). This new rendition of the old "way" could not be tolerated by a corrupted and politicized Judaism or an idolatrous and immoral Roman authority.

The first contest or war which would eventually transform the Roman Empire toward toleration of Christians, (prevailing of c-1) centers in the martyrdom of James and Peter.

James
Recent scholarship, especially on the Dead Sea Scrolls, has expanded our knowledge about the life and witness of Jesus' brother. He was killed for

his faith and rectitude by temple authorities and his martyr's death was thought for centuries to be the reason for the destruction of the temple and the fall of Jerusalem to the Romans. What do we know about James? Like John the Baptist he was a reformist Jew calling for a pure faith and an authentic ethic. His radical-restorative message was a condensation of prevalent Hasidic practice. With the Essenes he seems to have seen the present religious and political regime as corrupt. As we know from James' letter his messianic wisdom encompassed faith and works. It seemed at variance with the disjunction of those gifts which the apostle Paul would forward. Indeed until our new appraisals of the Judaising Paul there appeared to be a deep theological rift between these two formulators of Christ's faith.

Called "the Just One", the head of Jesus family (which seems to have been the core leaders of the resurrection church), and the first bishop among the Apostles, he exerted authority over the small Judeo-Christian and eventually the Gentile church of Paul and others:

- He prayed day and night and was said to have worn knees like a camel
- He led the economic efforts to sustain the famished poor of Judea (Paul's offering in Roman's)
- He preached his brother Jesus' resurrection and reign as Messiah and Lord

Eusebius writes at the time of Constantine:

> Unable to endure any longer the testimony of the
> Man, who on account of his elevated philosophy and
> religion, was deemed by all men to be the most
> righteous, they slew him...
> (quoted in Robert Eisenman, *James, the Brother of Jesus* (New York: Penguin, 1997), p. 414).

As Jesus' brother was thrown from the pinnacle of the temple, stoned and beaten to death with a fuller's brush, about this time the other James was beheaded. Accused of breaking Jewish law (blasphemy, adhering to the "Name" of Christ as God (c-3) and breaching Roman political order and peace, brother James' martyrial ("witnessing") ministry and death forms the background of the fate of the apostles Paul and Peter. It may be woven into the stoning of Stephen complex. Seeking to interrupt these times of tribulation in the preceding decade Paul had formulated a political theology of "the powers" which would ultimately shape the Christian view of the witness/martyr and its war ethic.

Paul on the "Powers"
The question is this: who is worthy of being honored and praised as King? This struggle seems to be at the root of the martyrdom both of the Jews under the Greeks and Romans and of the Christians under the Romans and Persians. Not only will the martyrs be "the seed of the church" (Gibbon), they will change the coming history, including military and political history, as the weight and undeniability of their witness eventually calls down the Roman empire, transforming it into the Byzantine and Holy Roman empires. Though initially faithful, as we shall see later, these empires fail to "get it" and by the crusades verge toward the demonic.

The crisis of the martyrs who live out the messianic "Name" against the powers of Rome, forms the backdrop for Paul's theology of the powers. Though deeply steeped in patriotism and proud of his Roman citizenship, Paul sees that honoring the governors and governments of this world will continually present a challenge to pure belief and practice. In his teaching he addresses both the form and substance (energy) of the powers. In his book *Christ and the Powers,* (Scottsdale: Herald, 1962) Hendrick Berkhof talks of the "principalities and powers" (Romans 12, 13) as:

Human traditions
Course of early life determined by stars
Fixed religious and ethical rules
The administration of justice and
Ordering of the state
The state
Politics
Class
Social struggle
National interest
Democracy
The clan
Ancestors
Family (p. 22, 25, 27)

For Paul as for Jesus and the apostles, the dawning of the new world (Jubilee) was also the twilight of this world. The powers of evil (*chäosmachte, weltmachte, bösemachte*) held sway over this fast-fading cosmos which was under anthroposatanic sway. By disarming the powers of "the world" the world of the flesh and the devil, a new cosmos *kaine ktisis*, a new creation could be fashioned. To accomplish this, godly forces must not only sweep the desolate cities and wretched death camps of Germany and the pacific Islands, not only parade those spoils and on

Hebrew Holy war heritage offer all to God, but declare truce and rebuild peace as in Marshall and MacArthur plans.

The *textus receptus* begins in Romans 12 and continues into 13, the great passage of political loyalty and acquiescence.

> 12:14 Bless those who persecute you; bless and do not curse them. 15 Rejoice with those who rejoice, weep with those who weep. 16 Live in harmony with one another; do not be haughty, but associate with the lowly; never be conceited. 17 Repay no one evil for evil, but take thought for what is noble in the sight of all. 19 Beloved, never avenge yourselves, but leave it to the wrath of God; for it is written, "Vengeance is mine, I will repay, says the Lord." 20 No, "if your enemy is hungry, feed him; if he is thirsty give him drink; for by so doing you will heap burning coals upon his head." 21 Do not be overcome by evil, but overcome evil with good.

> 13:1 Let every person be subjected to the governing authorities. For there is no authority except from God, and those that exist have been instituted by God. 2 therefore he who resists the authorities resists what God has appointed, and those who resist will incur judgment. 3 For rulers are not a terror to good conduct, but to bad. Would you have no fear of him who is in authority? Then do what is good, and you will receive his approval, 4 for he is God's servant for your good. But if you do wrong, be afraid, for he does not bear the sward in vain; he is the servant of God to execute his wrath on the wrongdoer. 5 Therefore one must be subject, not only to avoid God's wrath, but also for the sake of conscience.

Political and military issues throughout Christian history will pivot on these passages. In the church fathers they form the *raison d'être* for the doctrines of toleration, e.g. Clement and Tertullian, and eventually the Christian state (Augustine, Theodosius). In the Reformation they form the apologetics for critiquing the church/state and for justifying the resistance and wars of the reform princes.

This broad pericope of Paul's letter to Romans draws together the elements of renunciation, resistance and respect for the state. In chapter 12 we have the renunciation in Jesus' ethical teaching to "turn the other cheek", "love one's enemies", and "pray for those who persecute you". These texts are all the more amazing given the background of persecution. Resistance is also fostered by this passage as it extols that the State ultimately exists at God's allowance for His service. Finally we note the emphasis on good citizenship, obedience, and concession to the "power" of the State since she exists to hold "evil people" not the "good" under the sword of terror.

In 1964 I joined a cavalcade of clergy to the State of Mississippi to protest their frantic policies to deny African-Americans the right to vote. They passed new and expedient laws which required blacks to pass elaborate constitutional tests for suffrage, exacting far more stringent standards than they did for whites. We challenged those unjust laws by breaking other trumped up laws against picketing as we petitioned the local authorities. My home church in Pittsburgh was torn in its response to their young pastor. Some, including the senior minister, thought that I had violated Romans 13. I had not submitted to "higher authorities" which were "ordained by God". Others found my action fulfilling of Paul's doctrine of obedience and resistance to "power." Like all protest, resistance or aggression down the Christian ages, acts are always colored by uncertainty and ambivalence.

Such ambivalence will characterize the early church. As the day of Jesus and the Apostolic age fade into the bureaucratic age of the early church, faithfulness to the "war of the Lord" and the "War of the Lamb" will prove difficult. Enemies, once historical, then apocalyptic, like the "powers" in the Gospel and Epistle will sometimes be projected or distorted. Jews are hounded and ghettoized as the Diaspora seeks to survive in the now Christianized Constantinian empire. Abrahamic brothers are construed as mortal enemies as Islam arises and crusades respond. The first warm-up assault on Holy land Muslims is waged against Rhineland Jews who are herded into their synagogues and burned to death. Holy passion is contorted into vicious barbaric enmity. But before we chronicle this war saga in a later chapter let us consider one other salutary element of the early Christian campaign.

In a masterful sociological study of the early Christian movement Rodney Stark characterizes the belief system and action range by which, slowly but surely, Christianity wins over Roman philosophy and law as the faith/life perspective of the Roman Empire. It is a silent and, but for the violence against martyrs and gladiators, a bloodless coup (Rodney Stark, *The Rise of Christianity*, Princeton: Princeton University Press, 1996).

One central thesis in his study is that the belief in Christ's resurrection and resultant confidence in life beyond death leads to a creative and serene crucifixion theodicy (explanation of suffering) which, in turn, prompts an exemplary ministry of care for the sick and dying. Each of these beliefs, values and moral practices refutes and displaces a correlated pagan custom. For the Hellenistic-Roman world the gods were capricious and even the nobility of Platonic and Stoic immortality left one agonizingly in dread of death in a suicidal culture. Pain and suffering had to be denied as figmentary (neoplatonism) or serenely born as in the Stoics. There was no victory and no "good cheer" "I have overcome the world" (John 16:33). The ethics *sequellae* were even more grievous: infanticide, abortion, pederasty, suicide and a general neglect of nursing and compassion in favor of abandonment.

A second thesis Stark advances argues that it is not military conquest or even politically mediated coercion that extends the faith but a slow, natural evolutionary growth. In the same way that Mormons and some Pentecostal movements now multiply predictably (doubling every ten years) in the USA and the world so the early Christians proselytized their faith by their winsome manner of life and the efficacy of their programs of social service welfare, education, family life, healing and care for the destitute.

In a third thesis building on the pioneering work of Wayne Meeks (*The First Urban Christians*, Yale, 1983; *The Origins of Christian Morality*, Yale, 1993). Stark argues that the Christians found ways not only to tolerate but to transform and ameliorate the difficulties of urban existence. Anomie, poverty, work, hunger, friendship, security, muting of violence, family commitment, love of children, sanctuary for strangers and aliens were all issues addressed by the early Christian house fellowships, then churches, then bishop-cities. The successful provision for person's needs, especially those who were vulnerable and prone to exploitation proved to be the seal of success of Christianity in the empire.

The relevance to our thesis and to the war on terrorism must be evident. First, the early Christians, in living out the Decalogue/*akedic* manner of life contended the righteousness of God against the atheisms, idolatries and injustices of the pagan world. In quiet but convincing witness they won the war for souls, families, cities, kingdoms.

Today, radical political Islam, an ascending, albeit minority faith of some poor sectors of the world, has focused its righteous animosity, its holy passion, against the richest and most powerful nation in the world, the United States. Al Qaeda, Taliban and its sister movements, Lebanese Jihad, Egyptian brotherhood and numerous cognate groups in Pakistan, Palestine, Philippines, and the like flourish where the poor have been dispossessed and offended. The failure of these sometimes rich regimes (Saudi Arabia and the Arab Emirates) to provide for their own people's need is unconscionable. In other relatively poor countries; Iran, Iraq, Palestine, Egypt, Pakistan, the Philippines and the like, the state has not been able to provide adequate economic vitality or human services and radical Islamic movements have filled the void.

In Pakistan, for example, the 100,000 Madrasas – intense disciplined Islamic schools – are the only vital, dedicated centers of learning for poor desperate communities. Regrettably their curriculum is distorted Islam – violent, xenophobic, anti-American and anti-Semitic. Yet they alone offer educational discipline and care adequately for the needy.

The same was true for Afghanistan. The Taliban, despite their oppressive, no-fun regime (no kites, oppression and punishment of homosexuals, no school for girls, harsh dress codes for women), did care about more equitable economic sharing, diminishing the poppy industry and drug-trafficking, enhancing piety and family life. Again when all others ignored the poor they gave a damn – brutal though it was.

The war in our world today is for the souls of persons. Will the affluent West with its libertarian sexuality, its MTV indulgence, its fierce capitalist competition and its polarization of rich and poor – will the West, the decadent epicenter of Christian and Jewish faith – will it prevail? Only as she recovers justice and hope for the poor. Otherwise, she will continue to lose the war.

To illustrate the ironic yet strenuous contest for peace which is derived from the salient source of Abrahamic faith and ethics (Judaic, Christic, Islamic) in first century Palestine Michael Lerner, Liberal Rabbi, editor of *TIKKUN* offers a vision for peace in Israel-Palestine. Supplementing this crisis program with well-conceived preventions and well-envisioned prospectives would benefit any of those sixty some hot-spots in the world where terrorism defies establishment. I offer his proposal as fitting to our thesis.

A "reasonable" deal with the Palestinians would involve the following:

- Offer a Palestinian state in all of the land conquered in 1967, with only the slightest border changes to allow Israel to incorporate Gush, Etziyon, Ariel, and the sections of Jerusalem with a clear Jewish majority plus the Jewish section of the Old City and the Wall.
- Israel asks for a ban of heavy weapons (tanks and armed airplanes) and for the arrest of terrorists. To be policed by an international force created by the UN and given powers to ensure that terrorists are stopped. [my addition: this should include jurisdiction over terrorists on both sides].
- Israel shares Jerusalem, allowing the Palestinians full control over Palestinian sections of the city and unimpeded access to the Temple Mount. Without abandoning its claim to sovereignty over the Temple Mount, it gives Palestinians interim sovereignty until the messiah comes and Jews are once again allowed to use the Temple Mount (functional definition: "when nations beat their swords into ploughshares, make war no more, and the lion lies down with the lamb" as predicted by Isaiah).
- Israel offers compensation to any West Bank settlers who wish to resettle inside the pre-1968 Garden of Israel, and tells those who wish to remain outside the borders that they must live as peaceable citizens of the Palestinian state according to the laws of the

Palestinian state, and that Israel will not intervene if these settlers are charged with violation of Palestinian laws (including theft of Palestinian land).

- Israel agrees to spearhead, with the US and UN, a massive fund for reparations to Palestinian refugees, acknowledges partial (not total) responsibility for having caused the Palestinian refugee problem in 1948, and sets a yearly quota for return of refugees. ...Palestinians would have to agree to live in peace inside Israel, and Israel would have to end all discriminatory policies against Arabs (*de facto* as well as *de jure*).

- Both sides agree to end all propaganda demeaning Arabs, Jews, Islam and Judaism and to have their media and schools monitored and controlled on these issues by an international human rights organization (Editorial: "Can Colin Powell Rescue Us?" *Tikkun*, January, February 2002, p. 89).

We now need to leap forward to our contemporary world of religion and war. A movement of 500 years centered in Britain from Wyclif to Wesley offers further insight to our inquiry.

6
The Cousins' Wars

Historians note a peculiar iridescence of energy, power, aggression, even violence, that has arisen in Anglo-American culture in the modern era. Economic philosophers from Adam Smith (*The Wealth of the Nations*), Max Weber (*The Protestant Ethic and the Spirit of Capitalism*) and George Landes (*The Wealth and Poverty of Nations*) have observed this phenomenon. War historians like John Keegan and Victor Hanson have celebrated its political-military aspects. Radical Muslims identify it as a source of their iconoclastic resentment. I find a unique religious history spanning the five centuries from Wyclif to Wesley in England and chronicled in Kevin Phillip's *The Cousins' Wars* to be at the heart of this sometime divine, often demonic energy.

My plan in this chapter is to retrace the immediate precursors of the now-unfolding war of/on terrorism and the preceding modern wars for freedom against fascism and communism. I have in mind the span of what Kevin Phillip's calls *The Cousins' Wars*, enlarged to that Anglo-American saga ranging from Wyclif to Wesley and beyond the last Cousins' War (the American Civil War 1861-1865) to the turn of the twentieth century.

A Proviso
But first a commentary proviso. By now the reader will have felt the religio-political bias of the author which acknowledges a heart-felt remorse about the dark side of the colonialism, imperialism and even religious audacity which Anglo-America has visited on the world. As a young pastor during the Vietnam/US Civil Rights era I perfectly agreed with Dr. King that the domestic arrogance and oppression of African Americans was the flip side of the coin of American's misbegotten search for hegemony in Vietnam. So a critical appraisal of Kevin Phillip's *Cousins' Wars* comes hard for me. Yet to sustain my thesis of the mingled worthiness and unworthiness of extending the life and faith, in this case of American's Puritan religion, into the world, we can search out those godly and good

elements of the Anglo-American exertion in world history – therefore this chapter.

A new biography of Rudyard Kipling, *The Long Recessional* by David Gilmore (Farrar, Straus, Giroux, 2001) takes up the troubling legacy of the man who typified that noble yet perverse enterprise. Edward Said in his analysis of Kipling's *Kim* in *Culture and Imperialism* (Knopf, 1993) rightly called the novel "rich and absolutely fascinating" but "profoundly embarrassing" ("Kipling long ago envisioned what the U. S. may now learn," - Edward Rothstein, *New York Times*, January 26, 2002, p. A 19).

At century's turn Kipling argued that the U.S. (beginning its rule in the Philippines) should "Take up the White Man's Burden." This extended his thesis that the enlightened white race should rescue with faith and culture those "new-caught, sullen peoples/half devil and half child". Now in Afghanistan (the backdrop of much of Kipling's writing about the Khyber Pass) the US will confront the *denouement* of it's own ambivalent imperialism, contends Rothstein. We will need to sort out the salutary from the deleterious side of our global intentions and interventions. Just as in Israel today we must distinguish our honorable call to secure and defend global Israel from the extermination began in Christian crusades and European Holocaust from own unworthy complicity in her vicious oppression of Palestinians, we must also distinguish good from evil now in the war on terrorism. Rothstein's words are telling (decalogic and *akedic*):

> Kipling, of course was sure of Britain's cultural superiority as indeed, America is of its own when confronted with the Taliban. But Kipling suggests that the superiority also entails sacrifice. All "profit and gain", he asserts in his poem (*The Man Who Would Be King*) must be sought not for oneself but for the other. Famine and sickness must be eliminated. Battles for peace must be waged. But nothing should be expected in return…In the poem's imagery, the end of naïve childhood for the conquered is also the weary end of the naïve childhood for the conqueror. (P.A. 19)

Thus forewarned let us first rehearse our thesis: I have argued that Abrahamic history sets in motion a religious fervor – a theology and ethics or beliefs and behaviors – which shape not only the parochial but the public ethos of Judaism, Christianity and Islam. This gives shape to what I have called a protestantization of values and a contention for goods which undergirds and overlays the war history of the past two millennia, including the present war on terrorism. Befitting this descriptive thesis is also a normative thesis which finds ethical legitimacy in the "rightful" wars for "decalogic/*akedic*" truth and good but finds illegitimacy in contests for any other values. Maintenance of justice-grounded peace is the bedrock issue.

To sharpen this thesis at the outset of a section in Anglo-American war theology, let me review the arguments of a colleague philosopher-moralist, Michael Novak. In an essay in *National Review* (Dec 31, 2001) he writes of the characteristics of "A Nation That Believes":

- A close relation of reason and faith
- Recognition that the nation originated in Jewish and Christian faith
- Recognition of the dynamics of faith heritage which "ignites new awakenings and fosters new births of struggle and reformation" (p. 32).
- Life and liberty are conjoined (interdependent) gifts of God
- Slavery or oppression are intolerable "at home" or "out there" in the world "God's justice cannot sleep forever" (T. Jefferson)
- Inextricable relation of truth and freedom "the truth shall make you free" (Gospel of John)
- Ultimate truth (God) undergirds penultimate truths of practical life: education, politics, science, law
- Faith also compels us to "care for the widow and orphan"
- The dignity of each person must undergird national and international piety
- The encounters with God in "spirit and truth" grounds liberty and righteousness (p. 31, 32)

My thesis in this work is not as rational and Thomistic ("natural law") driven as Michael Novak's nor is it as univocally patriotic. He is a grateful catholic compatriot; I am a critical Puritan compatriot. My contention is that faith and ethics are perceived and conceived (received and self-affirmed) in all dimensions of being: rational, emotional, physical and social. But I do generally follow Novak's convictions: faith → freedom → responsibility. I believe that truth and good are not only "naturally endowed" and teleologically drawn, they are revealed, learned, worked at and fought for. As his colleague writer in *The Nation*, William Buckley Jr. would comment from his similarly Aristotelian sensibility, reason might say "my country, right or wrong" – faith might say "confirmed in right, criticized in wrong". This more dialectical posture would arise from my argument.

The *Cousins' Wars* traces the origins of this world view. From some five million persons on England's Eastern Coast, West Country and Wales, along with some 50,000 like minded Puritan pilgrims to North America, has arisen a way of looking at the world, a way of conceiving war, a way of perceiving and living out national destiny, a religio-politic which has changed the world. Indeed those religious perspectives and geopolitics are interdependent. To trace the war history, the underlying theology and the current legacy of this people and its project is the task of this chapter. I will seek to distill the essence of this Anglo-American heritage, showing how it conveys and also distorts our biblical norm, and so buttresses the argument of this essay. We will finally note the elements which contribute to war and terrorism and conversely to justice and peace.

Some of the equivocal and ambivalent elements in this tradition are:

- The manifest destiny of this people as part of "God's chosen" to work out His "way" in the world.
- The construal of this "way" as involving evangelism, colonization, strife, even war, though ultimately peace.
- The contention is characterized by a suspicion of the "state church" and "Catholicism," as well as of all religio-ecclesial patriotism.
- The commitment therefore is to freedom, democracy, toleration and attention to the weak, vulnerable, laborers, women and children of a society, and for strangers and sojourners.
- An Abrahamic/*akedic* paradigm for national and religious life entailing a sense of "chosenness", "holy passion", obligation, responsibility and judgment.
- An evangelical/apocalyptic political/theology which sees in historical crises the presentation of this divine judgement and the call therefore for repentance, resistance and ultimately, concord.

The war history of Anglo-American Protestants
A strain of religious public philosophy which is embodied in the faith of George W. Bush (much more than his New England Patrician father), Vice-President Cheney and other close advisors, typified by Southeastern and Southwestern American Methodists, can be traced for its roots in the "Cousins'," transferred to this "new land," and to the grounding religio-ethical formation of the "Cousins' Wars." While sympathetic public ethos is found in Scots-Irish immigrants of the 18th and 19th centuries, by Palatinate German, Scandinavian and even Irish catholic émigrés, the salient and constitutive world-view and "Holy passion" of the USA in the twenty first century is that conveyed by the transgenerational community which fought the English civil war against the British crown in the American Revolution against lingering colonial oppression, and in the US Civil war (on both sides, but primarily with the Union against slavery).

These three English speaking civil wars, argues Phillips, are wars of religion. They are wars which not only arise from religious convictions and commitments, but they fashion a people and nation which will constitute and guide the present "Lingua Anglicana", the global evolution of communication policies and economics forming the "global community and world hegemony" (p. xi). The bifurcation of the English speaking world into two communities one "aristocratic", "chosen" and "imperial" and one democratic, "chosen" and "manifest destiny driven" (p. xi) is, to my mind, the decisive political development underlying not only those three "English civil wars" but the "rightful" (decalogic/*akedic*) and "questionable" wars of the twentieth and twenty-first centuries which we have considered. Discerning, therefore, this war heritage for its salutary and deleterious aspects will help us assess the presently ongoing "war on terrorism." Religion is a two-edged sword. It animates the finest and most "God-like" human endeavors. It also "…can be a tool to reinforce diseased perceptions of reality" [Rowan Williams, the archbishop of Wales was lecturing at Trinity Church, New York, just meters from the World Trade Center on September 11. His moving reflections (especially on "war") are found in *Writing in the Dust: After September 11*, (Grand Rapids: Eerdmans, 2002) 5].

Let us again, with Phillips' help, list the fundamental tenants of their faith/way:

- Distinctive (ascetic, frugal) lifestyle
- Biblical study
- Synergy of careful Bible reading and sermons constituted "Word" of God for life
- Predestinarian theory
- Suspicion of Rome
- Sabbatarians
- English peoples or evangelical (reborn) Christians wherever were "chosen people"
- Elect body (for worldly mission)
- Fear of losing salvation through moral or missional shortcomings
- Perdition of the lost—missionary imperative
- Opposed to Apostolic authority but obedient to biblical authority
- Ethical reformists (e.g. drunkenness, indolence, debauchery, revels and other "fun" (p. 20)

"Our God," sings English, British then American religious nationalism, is a "God of War." From Handel's Messiah to New England sermons, this mischievous phrase echoes. Yet a subtle internal logic should allow us to discern with Israel when God fights for us (*Gott mit uns*) and when God fights against us. Torah and messiah is God's war for the world with or against his people. Even in these wars, as Karl Barth often reflected, we see the glory and tragedy of "human life under God". The fratricide of the US civil war is particularly poignant for several reasons. First, as President Bush affirmed this morning, at the funeral of the first American "Green Beret" killed (accidentally) in Afghanistan, "It was just".

Surely the war between the North and the South served justice. Can one imagine a more despicable atrocity than the North American slave trade and the national disgrace depicted in the book *Roots* (Alex Haley)? That slavery surely equals in cruelty the founding and grievous act of dispossession and genocide of the aboriginal American people. These two evils and mysterious divine judgments on them form the archaic disgrace from which America must repent if she is to become God's *avant garde* in the world.

The ambivalent history of the "white man's power" assertion in the world confronts our consciousness today. As with the Cherokee and Miami nations in the USA, in the war of terrorism we confront traditional tribal peoples, these shaped by primitive Islam, especially in the indigenous peoples of Afghanistan. The overlay of a rich, Arab playboy ethic, full of resentment and violence, embodied by the likes of Osama bin Laden, complicates the justice discernment of this war on terrorism.

In the war on terrorism, American power is being forced to confront her historic ambition to take, occupy and coercively influence the lands of other peoples. The historic colonial evils behind the war on terrorism is America's hegemony in Arabia enforcing its interest in cheap oil and the implantation of Israel in Palestine in response to the Christian genocide of European Jews. The attack on September 11 of seventeen martyrdom-bound Arab tribesmen, incubated in a conflict originating in Afghanistan where Saudi Arabian, Pakistani, Yemeni, and Palestinian refugees found range for their ideas and actions, was further funded and nurtured in European cities – Hamburg, London and trained in flight schools in Florida. When the planes plunged in to the twin towers that morning, could we but remember the 24-dollar purchase, by Dutch Calvinist colonels of Manhattan Island below, from other aboriginal peoples.

Kevin Phillips offers the following historical thesis in this Cousins' Wars:

> ...From the seventeenth century, the English-speaking peoples on both continents defined themselves by wars that upheld, at least for a while, a guiding political culture of a low church, Calvinistic Protestantism, commercially adept, militarily expansionist and highly convinced in the Old World, New World or both, that it represented a chosen people and a manifest destiny" (p. xv).

When George W. Bush stands with Tony Blair, British Prime Minister, arm in arm announcing the war on terrorism, we see the legacy of this history.

Three "puritanisms", suggests Phillips, underlie the three Cousins' wars. Those "puritanisms," I suggest are shaped by our English religious tradition which runs from Wyclif to Wesley. "Puritanism" is a name applied to the sixteenth and seventeenth century expression of a long-evolving world view. Following its roots in biblically/literalistic and apocalyptic Judaism, Reformism begins with radical Catholics in the middle ages: the Franciscans, Waldensians, Rhineland mystics, Albegensians, Hussites and others. It continues in the vitalities of the English puritans, the other nonconformists: Baptists, Quakers, pietists and the like. It culminates in the Wesleyan movement. The "Puritan" ingredients were the desire to purify or restore a pristine faith and way of life; to secure a greater holiness amid the worldliness and corruption of the domain and body; to tear away from a too-easy accommodation with government; to reform the church-state relation into a doctrine of complementary relation according to Calvin; to listen to and obey what the voice of God (prophetic scripture) enjoined for the social order and to convey this "reformed" view nationally and internationally. It was an epoch of reenactment of the trials and errors of biblical Israel.

The puritan movement in the 16th and 17th centuries includes the age of the Marian martyrs (recall Foxe's book), the arousal of biblical preaching and tyrannicidal policies under Cromwell, and the eventual settlement back in to a more reformed church-state nation under the Stuarts. The fervor and "Holy passion" generated by the puritans and other non-conformists are transplanted to New England in the pilgrim plantation and the subsequent Scots-Irish emigration. It continues in England and in North America in the Great Awakening and the Wesleyan movement.

And today. Kevin Phillips comments that by 1950 Americans were consenting their will with ballots just as their cousins two, three, four, five and six centuries earlier had with bullets. Even the year 2000 disputed election of George W. Bush follows the geographical demography of the cousins campaign. Though Gore won the popular vote, the red and blue national map was telling. Gore prevailed only in the three great megalopolises: San (Diego) -Seattle, Chi-troit (Chicago-Detroit) and Bo-wash (Boston-Washington). The rest of the country – the heartland – the Methodist, Baptist, Presbyterian heartland—was all Bush. Almost half of the US population now lives in these strip cities. The rural states which voted Bush were the successors to the old cousins' war – white holy warriors.

The English Civil War
The English Civil War provides the setting for the Westminster assemblies (1640's) which formulated the Westminster confession of faith and catechisms. These texts have undergirded Presbyterian and Baptist belief and action for three centuries. Perceptively, as George III identified the colonial enemy he saw himself and the empire fighting against "the Presbyterian commonwealth."

R.H. Tawney, early in the 20th century, recognized the connection between religion and the Puritan cultural endeavor in areas like economics, politics and international relations. In *Religion and the Rise of Capitalism* he showed that "the growth, triumph and transformation of the Puritan spirit was the most fundamental movement of the seventeenth century...(This) was the true English reformation" (New York: Mentor, 1954, p. 165).

This development in English history was corroborated by three parallel movements prior to the civil war which strengthened the ethos which would shape the character of Anglo-Americans: to the North the Scots convention had formulated in 1638 a "Solemn Covenant", at one level a liturgical and ecclesiastical movement concerned with the Prayer Book and the liturgy. At the same time they mustered an army at the border of England. *Ora et Labora* became *Ora et Bella*. In the West the Scots and Scots – Irish were forming what would become the second great wave of immigration to America (along with "Reformed" Germans from the Palatinate). Finally, in the colonies themselves the English Puritans (pilgrims) fashioned a radical political ethos together with their more ecclesial establishmentarians.

The American War of Independence
The moral legacy of the American Revolutionary War is also profound and far-reaching. Standing in the noble yet ambitious heritage of the sequence of Western Wars of Revolution – English (1640's), French (1780's), German (1840's), Russian (1910's) – the joyous yet furious impulses of freedom are released – yet a range of tragic determinisms will follow.

Scholars like Frances Fukiyama argue that liberty has become infectious and victorious, undermining all tyrannies and collectivities in its irresistible energy. Freedom is the imperative of the first three commandments: God alone, no idols, true confession. It is anchored in the *akedic* miracles of righteousness fulfilled where life and resurrection overwhelms evil and death. Freedom in other words, only exists in the context of decalogic responsibility. If freedom deteriorates into libertinism in the aftermath of the French Revolution, its very freedom is lost. If the social justice and solidarity of the communist revolution abandons respect for individual liberty, it loses its social justification.

The American Revolution becomes a paradigm of the grand universal experiment in freedom. It's experience will inspire revolutions from China and Vietnam at mid-century, to African and South American aspirations at the dawn of the 21st century. Fukiyama and Milton Friedman are also correct in that that political event exists in the ethos of democratic and human rights commitments and of the global economy.

Today as Argentina's economy languishes as it dissociates from the dollar standard and as American-led IMF and world bank "free enterprise" requirements become suspect in their efficacy, we continue to wonder whether "liberty" will bring forth the fruits of justice. The ancient questions raised by an "Axis of Terror" (Chapter 5) and of terrible freedom in Paul of Tarsus (Galatians 5) still haunt the world. These questions of causality and "justice for all" are the tests of that freedom which derives from the biblical tradition.

The American Civil War
Finally it is in the American Civil War that the moral excellence and the moral ambiguity of the Puritan war ethic become clear. Phillips develops his discussion of this final Cousins' war in two chapters:

1. Sectionalism, slavery and religion
2. The final Cousins' fight: the U.S. Civil War

One of the unfortunate results of the Revolutionary War was that it cut loose the restraint on removal of the Native Americans and the extension of slavery westward. The Republican Party arose against these insidious movements in the Kansas-Nebraska Act of 1854. This break with the move prevalent acquiescence to slavery set the stage for the American Civil War. The language and rhetoric of "liberty" became more and more obviously discordant with actual custom and policy. As in most wars, even the second world war, where many people did not feel totally comfortable with the loss of nationalistic fascism, in the aftermath of the Revolution many found that they were not really enthused by the implied quality and emancipation of subordinates and slaves.

The "Negrophobic" doctrine of black inferiority, fears of protecting the "white woman," notions of property rights and residual prejudice – all concepts firmly believed by some to be enhanced in free choice – rubbed against the new ethos, especially if that were to be legally imposed.

Theologically speaking, not only did high-church Anglicans and Anglo-catholic Methodists and Presbyterians hesitate to accept radical liberation, but conservative political tendencies and fear of change in more evangelical circles amplified the hesitation.

As with the value clarification and elucidation which followed the American revolution, so too the Civil War forced the United States to clarify its central decalogic values. For example, is opportunity, equality and sharing goods with the poor (C-1, C-4, C-8) a preeminent value over the sacrosanctity of property (C-9, C-10)? This discernment is the same as that I call for in this volume to identify legitimate and illegitimate wars. "Liberty and justice for all" may require constraint of freedom and an increase of responsibility on my part. That is threatening.

To trace the theological ingredients of the Cousins' Wars in general and in the United States Civil War in particular we must remember that each war was preceded by a powerful religious revival. The rise of Puritanism and its precursor Protestant Reformation was the most profound moment of religious vitality since the Pauline revolution in the early church and the Augustinian renewal in the fourth century. The latter two Cousins' wars were preceded by and, we might argue, were precipitated by, the first and second Great Awakening.

In Phillips' interesting and provocative words, "each time, three or four decades of rising religious excitement and political contention were necessary to beat plowshares and candlesticks back into swords" (p. 357). He goes on to find the First Great Awakening (and the American Revolution) based on the First Commandment and the Second based on the second table. If the very freedom of faith and liberation from tyranny animated the Revolution, humanistic concerns of loving and improving the neighbor (C-5-10) underlay the United States Civil War.

Seeking justice and redress of the inhumanity of slavery was one impulse of the third "Puritan" war. Abstinence and moral reform was another. The great temperance movements in Illinois and Massachusetts were constraints rising from the awakening. In Evanston, Illinois for example Methodist revivalism led to the WCTU. In many ways these moral reforms were intermediate stages between the experience of salvation and the ensuring strife of war. At the same time in the 1840's and 1850's persons like Eliza Garrett, Frances Willard, Susan B. Anthony and Elizabeth Cady Stanton pioneered not only restoration from debauchery to being chaste warriors for men but also leadership and renewed dignity for women. The exact ritual of Holy war in Israel (Deuteronomy 20) was reenacted where personal chastity and marital fidelity were the behavioral conditions for victorious war. Only Holy passion could succeed.

Phillips concludes:

> ...In Massachusetts, Walt Whitman wrote of drums beating and warlike America rising. Charles Eliot Norton called the cause 'a religious war...a man must carry with him the assurance that he is acting in the immediate presence and as the commissioned soldier of God.' Oliver Wendell Holmes penned the "Army Hymn", described as 'a fervent appeal to the Puritan God of battles', (I heard it played today as 12 soldiers wounded in Kandahar received purple hearts) Phillips continues: "even Quaker poet John Greenleaf Whittier penned a new version of *"Ein feste Burg ist unser Gott"* (p. 362).

Mingled within the slavery issue was the issue of free-labor and economics. In my own ancestral land of Pennsylvania the world's first oil well kicked in in the early 1860's, and countless seams of rock-hard black anthracite fired in the furnaces as warrior steel, however crude, was refined. The rails of the Carnegies and Mellons would speed all to its intended use. In the 1870's my great grandfather from Northern Pennsylvania floated hardwood logs down the Clarion and Allegheny rivers to Pittsburgh, then walked the 80 miles back home. These very likely built the elegant confederate plantation homes further down the Ohio and Mississippi river. The war's outcome would rest on effective labor, markets and inspired industry.

Economic values intertwine deeply with religious values. Indeed it may be argued in light of the commands about theft, lying, coveting and the like, that economic values are religious values. The United States Civil War was much about such religio-economic issues. So, of course, are all wars, "If the Kuwaitis product was oranges (not oil)" said Secretary Baker during the Gulf War, "there would be no fuss". Commerce, piracy, tariffs, slaves, debts, and the working class were prominent issues in the war. Mercantile cotton interests were behind both slavery in the confederacy and in the desire to expand cotton farming with the decision to concentrate the Cherokee, Choctaw, and Seminole tribes for the same reason.

One interesting comparison/contrast of the Afghanistan war against the Taliban and the United States Civil War is the linkage between personal behavioral vice and social justice concerns. We have shown the 19th century connection between evangelical and ethical concern (drunkenness, smoking, dancing, etc.). In Afghanistan the puritanical Taliban led by fervent Mullahs, demanded sexual and marital fidelity, levied harsh shariah law against stealing and sought to suppress poppy growth, drug trafficking and drug use. The American engagement inspired by Puritan Wars I, II, II is therefore conflicted. It too seeks such values. Family, fidelity and public good values are important. But the primary values behind and in those earlier wars were liberty, freedom, constitutional rights and tyrannicide—libertarian values somewhat incompatible with Puritan values.

Concluding this chapter on the Cousins' wars we move from descriptive to normative reflection. Six weeks before his assassination Abraham Lincoln delivered a speech for the ages in his Second Inaugural. It develops the theology of terror and war and of justice and peace.

On the occasion corresponding to this four years ago, all thoughts were anxiously directed to an impending civil-war. All dreaded it—all sought to avert it. While the inaugural address was being delivered from this place, devoted all together to saving the Union without war, insurgent agents were in the city seeking to destroy it without war—seeking to dissol[v]e the Union, and divide effects, by negotiation. Both parties deprecated war, but one of them would *make* war rather than let the nation survive; and the other would *accept* war rather than let it perish. And the war came.

One eighth of the whole population were colored slaves, not distributed equally over the whole Union, but localized in the Southern part of it. These slaves constituted a peculiar and powerful interest. All knew that this interest was, somehow, the cause of the war. To strengthen, perpetuate, and extend this interest was the object for which the insurgents would rend the Union, even by war; while the government claimed no right to do more than restrict the territorial enlargement of it. Neither party expected for the war, the magnitude or the duration, which it has already attended. Neither anticipated that the *cause* of the conflict might cease with, or even before, the conflict itself. Each looked for an easier triumph and a result less fundamental and astounding. Both read the same Bible, and pray to the same God; and each invokes His aid against the other. It may seem strange that any men should dare to ask a just God's assistance in wringing their bread from the sweat of other men's faces, but let us judge not that we be not judged. The prayers of both could not be answered; that of neither had been answered fully. The Almighty has his own purposes. "Woe unto the world because of offenses! For it must needs be that offences come; but woe to the man by whom the offence cometh!" If we shall suppose that American Slavery is one of those offences which, in the providence of God, must need come, but which, having continued through His appointed time, He now wills to remove, and that He gives to both North and South, this terrible war, as the woe due to those by whom the offence came, shall we discern therein any departure from those divine attributes which the believers in a Living God always ascribe to Him? Fondly we do hope—fervently do we pray—that this mighty scourge of war may speedily pass away. Yet, if God wills that it continue, until all the wealth piled by the bond-man's two hundred and fifty years of unrequited toil shall be sunk, and until every drop of blood drawn with the lash shall be paid by another drawn with the sword, as was said three thousand years ago, so still it must be said "the judgements of the Lord, are true and righteous altogether."

> With malice toward none; with charity for all; with firmness in the right, as God gives us to see the right, let us strive on to finish the work we are in; to bind up the nations wounds; to care for him who shall have borne the battle, and for his widow, and his orphan—to do all which may achieve and cherish a just, and a lasting peace, among ourselves, and with all nations (Carl Sandburg, *Abraham Lincoln: the War Years*, Vol. 3, (New York: Dell, 1954)).

In the speech, which Frederick Douglass called "A Sacred Effort," Lincoln sought in this address national focus on the will of God in the war. Inspired by a letter from abolitionist preacher Henry Ward Beecher, just two weeks before the Inaugural "...peace can come only by arms," he opened the Bible to Isaiah 5: 27-28:

> none shall be weary nor stumble among them; none shall slumber nor sleep; neither shall the girdle of their loins be loosed, nor the latchet of their shoes be broken. Whose arrows are sharp, and all their bows bent, their horses' hoofs shall be counted like flint, and their wheels like a whirlwind.

This text again interprets the weary conclusion of the war in terms of the Hebrew exile remnant returning to 'bind up the wounds" and "...achieve and cherish a just and lasting peace..." Just as the founders of the country signaled the impossibility of continuing slavery in their commitment to liberty and equality, and just as some Americans forsook that founding charter, the way that Israel had forsaken its decalogic charter, so now the "righteous judgements' of the "living God' must be faced in the censure and cleansing of war.

Regarding the war, Lincoln says that while all persons sought to "avert" it others chose to "make" war, forcing the remainder to "accept" war. Here the "good" at stake is the "indissoluble union", the political covenant, which Lincoln, from the Gettysburg Address on, saw as a human compact under God. To "destroy" this union, this freedom, this republic, required "accepting" the great evil of war. The success of the Southern states sought to "destroy" the nation was as improbable as that of the seventeen suicide bombers of September 11 to destroy "freedom" or the "American way of life". It is unlikely that the "confederate terrorists" held such a lofty and abstract ambition. Their objective was more modest. They sought to preserve certain "ways of life" which they associated with liberty and the American way. They sough to find a way out of a confining box. They sought to resist the dominion of the Northern states.

Lincoln now moves to the theological heart of his argument. Here he is profoundly cognizant of the mistaken fury and the unholy zeal attending both camps. He is aware of the refracted sight, the obscure revelation, the ambiguous motives and the besetting frailty of all humans. He focuses now on the ultimate evil of slavery: "All knew that this interest was, somehow, the cause of the war." Behind the religious impulses of equality and the freedom the concrete case puts values to the test. Lincoln's candor is honed by the suffering of the war. At its outset he played down slavery and emphasized union. Similarly today we reprise to acknowledge:

- that the war on terrorism is about religion,
- that its epicenter is Israel, and

- that our interests in the region are complex including further craving for cheap oil to satiate our consumption.

Lincoln continues with the sobering realization that war brings much more than we had bargained for. It spirals out of control so that, in the end, as with a lawsuit, none are winners, and all (except the lawyers) are losers.

> Neither party expected for the war, the magnitude, or the duration, which it has already attained. Neither anticipated that the cause of the conflict might cease with, or even before, the conflict itself should cease. Each looked for an easier triumph and a result less fundamental and astounding.

As he stated in his early reflection on "Just War," Augustine reminded Christendom and all humanity that the furious cascade of war will carry all along to destruction in its wake. For this reason, vengeance, brutal violence toward others, even bully belligerence (pride) had no place in just and holy war. As soon as the motives and satisfactions turn to such ugly and unholy passion we should desist from conflict.

The discussion of slavery now has an almost sublime justice and righteousness. No longer do we feel retribution or hurt. Here we at last rise to a word Lincoln defines: "Magnanimity" and we come close to Portia's words in Merchant of Venice: "we humans are most like God when mercy tempers justice."

Lincoln recalls the wisdom of Thomas Jefferson growing out of the sanctifying instruction of the Revolution. In his 1787 Query XVIII from Notes on the State of Virginia, he writes:

> There must doubtless be an unhappy influence on the manners of our people produced by the existence of slavery among us... The man must be a prodigy who can retain his manners and morals undepraved by such circumstances. And with what execration should the statesman be loaded, who permitting one half of the citizens thus to trample on the rights of the other, transforms those into despots, and these into enemies, destroys the morals of the one part, and the amor patriae of the other...

Indeed I tremble for my country when I reflect that God is just: that his justice cannot sleep forever: that considering the number, nature and natural means only, a revolution of the wheel of fortune, an exchange of situation, is among possible events: that it may become probable by supernatural interference! The Almighty has no attribute which can side with us in such a contest (Lucas E. Morel, *Lincoln's Sacred Effort* (Lanham: Lexington Books, 2000) 176, 195).

As with Jefferson, Lincoln looked into the ambiguous heart of religion, seeing its beauty and sufficiency and its ugliness and danger. In the great civil war and in our present war on terrorism those finer and baser impulses ought to come to fore.

In six weeks Lincoln was killed by a crazed and indoctrinated actor. Like Anwar Sadat of Egypt or Yitzak Rabin of Israel, he became an akedic martyr. Living for the right he became a sacrifice, gathering the animosity and injustice from the past and the justice, hope and peace from the future into one redemptive proleptic act of mercy.

...greater love hath no man than this.

Conclusion

The only protection against self-righteousness is the consciousness that you too stand under the judgement of God and history. As Cromwell pleaded before Parliament and Assembly "...Brethren, I beseech you by the bowels of Christ, consider it possible that you may be mistaken." The only safe *Imperium* is a self-deprecating *Imperium*. This is the national self-consciousness of a nation who witnesses "In God We Trust." The three Cousins' or Puritan Wars pursue this fine-grained equipoise. The great wars against tyranny in Europe bear out this benign spirit. The wars against communism continue that rightful effort but begin to assume power-based self-justification and more grievously the deification of capitalism and right-wing political order (this especially in South America and Asia). The war(s) against terrorism now tests this ambiguity. We now turn to a deeper religious calamity—the dissociation and trifurcation of the Abrahamic faith heritage—to further clarify where we have been in order to see where we are and where we must go.

7

The fatal trifurcation

Listen to me, O coastlands
Pay attention peoples from far away
You are my servant Israel
In whom I will be glorified.
I will give you as a light to the nations
That my salvation may reach to the end of the earth.
Psalm 49

Ragged Israel limps back from exile only to hear that her noble destiny continues even in weakness and humiliation. Indeed, in deeper mystery she learns that her humiliation *is* exaltation.

This mystery of divine providence lies in the deep background of the war on terrorism. Why has the Abrahamic family of faiths converged and diverged as it has traversed history? Why does Christianity emerge within the bosom of the faith/life of Israel only to sever itself and find itself severed from its maternal source? Why then does the Seventh Century struggle for purity of faith and life lead to the rising of Islam and to such a fatal trifurcation of Abraham's legacy? And why the perpetual animosity? Why do Israelis today bulldoze homes of Palestinian Muslims in Gaza leaving them dead and homeless? Why do Christian Serbs massacre and bury alive Kosovan Muslims? Why do Muslims plow their hijacked planes into brothers and sisters of their own faiths in the World Trade Center? Why this fratricidal rage? We deal with blasphemy in this trifurcation—negating siblings who bear and live by the same name.

As I asked a panel of Jewish and Christian scholars recently at the Society of Christian Ethics meeting in Vancouver, how long will Jewish, Christian and Muslim ethics continue to create "moral agony" in the world as:

- Jews occupy Palestine and oppress its people
- Christians inflict the "dark side" of imperial crusade in the demand for political hegemony, the global economy, and the biomedical project
- Muslims terrorize with suicidal violence?

In Arabia, Islam plays the same transformative function that Christianity played in Abyssinia. The Monophysite Church of Syria and the Christianized kingdom of Axum helped shape a Judaic tribal theology and culture which took on "divine state" aspects and as directly influenced Islam.

Muslims probably derive from the Semitic-Jewish-Christians who disappeared into history with the Roman Shoah (66-73 CE). In 615 CE proto-Muslims asked the Ethiopian king for refuge. Legend has it that the Ethiopian king asked why they abandoned their people and homeland yet did not flee either to Christian or Jewish faith. In a passage crucial to the Quran and the Hadith literature they answered:

> ...a barbarous nation, worshipping idols, eating carrion, committing shameful deeds, killing our blood relations, forgetting our duty towards our neighbors, the strong among us devouring the weak. Such was our state until God sent us an apostle, from amongst ourselves, with whose lineage, integrity, trustworthiness and purity of life we were aquatinted. He summoned us to God, to believe in His unity, to worship Him and abandon the stones and idols...He commanded us to speak the truth, to be faithful in our trusts, to observe our duties to our kinsfolk and neighbors, to refrain from forbidden things and bloodshed...from consuming the property of orphans and from slandering virtuous women. He ordered us to worship God and associate no other with Him, to offer prayer, give alms and fast...So we trusted in his word and followed the teachings he brought us from God...Wherefore our countrymen turned against us and persecuted us to try and seduce us from our faith, that we might abandon the worship of God and return to the worship of idols (Arend Van Leewen, *Christianity on World History,* New York: Scribners, p. 73).

The stringent, strict, even severe monolatry, iconoclasm and morality of Islam would join with the shortsightedness of both Judaism and Christianity to tear their simple conjoined fabric of a pure and wise faith and life into three parts. When Jesus sends his apostles only to the lost sheep of Israel (Matthew 10:6) or addresses God in Aramaic as *El'lah*, we see the synthetic character of these faiths. Looked at in one way Islam saw its arrival as a reformation and renewal of Judeo-Christianity. These faiths had fallen into disrepair, idolatry and immorality. She also positions herself firmly in the traditions of *tarut* (Torah) and *injil* (Gospel). In rejection, reform and recapitulation of her two parental faiths she moans internally and externally to both propel the monotheistic movement and to go it on her own.

The first tragic dimension of the trifurcation is the rejection of Islam by Judaism. Muhammad wanted to stay within Judaism. Though he did not know the Torah he revered what he knew by hearing. Incorporation into Judaism was natural. There was a universal custom of circumcision in ancient Arabia. Islam was patterned after Judaism. Abraham is the progenitor of the faith. The *akedah* (sacrifice of Isaac) was the paradigmatic center of the sin, forgiveness, redemption complex in Islam. They observed the Sabbath. The Jewish Day of Atonement arises from this matrix as the fast of *Ashûrâ*. Most of the festivals were taken over. The Noachian commandments (Genesis 9) are central as they were with Pauline Christianity.

Regrettably, a defensive and embattled Judaism, still fresh from Roman persecutions, did not accept Muslims as "God-fearers." Like the New Testament, Muslim teaching objects to the detailed Kosher customs. Still Muhammad appeals for rapprochement with Jews and Christians, sibling faiths in the Book.

> Say; O People of the Book, come to the word which is
> Fair between us and you, that we serve no one
> But God, that we associate nothing with Him, and
> That none of us take as Lords 'beside God'
> (Quran, Surah III.57)

Islam's stated destiny according to the prophet is to mediate the contention between Judaism and Christianity restoring the unity of the faith family of Abraham. The crux of the argument goes this way:

> The Rabbis say:
> "Among the 'goyim' there are righteous who (belong) to the world
> to come."

> Quran says:
> "...and in the world to come he (Abraham) shall be among the
> just."

> Paul to Romans (2:14, 4:9 ff) says:
> "When the Gentiles did the law by nature, they are a law unto
> themselves."

"Faith was reckoned to Abraham as righteousness."

How can this noble purpose be squared with September 11? Only in this way. The crucial story of the two precursor faiths is a love that reaches across eternity to earth, rescues a lost humanity in a sacrificial death (Passover, *akedah*, the Crucifixion) in order to unite that which was severed apart.

> ...He has broken down the dividing wall between us
> He is our peace who has made the two, one
> By giving his body on the cross he broke the enmity (Ephesians 2).

The death of 3,000 plus innocents in the World Trade Center, of some dozens in the *akedic* sacrificial crash on the same day north of Pittsburgh, and of the seventeen terrorists fanatically following the brutal violence of other conspirators like Osama bin Laden (cf. Judas and his sponsors) may be the *akedic* offering which may make the twain or three, one.

On the eve of the World Trade Center calamity Jewish, Christian and Muslim leaders and followers gathered in hundreds of worship places, kneeling, crying, praying, beseeching, forgiving, admonishing and encouraging one another. Seldom, if ever had this happened before. Could this be the justice that could eventuate in peace? Could the Ka'bah, the black rock at the base of the "Dome of the Rock" in Jerusalem—where symbolically Abraham offered Isaac and the prophet ascended; where the wilderness akedic offerings now focused in the Jewish temple the sacrificial cult with all of the efficacy of Passover, Exodus, Jubilee, (the inner redemptive meaning of Israel); and where Jesus mounted his akedic tree (as the ram of Genesis 22) and died on the cross; could this be the citadel from which new life would be born? The great prophets of these three bodies say that here all peoples shall come to Zion. Here the nations shall break their swords into plowshares. Here all the nations of the world shall be blessed (Isaiah, Micah).

Kaa'bah says Quran was "The first house founded for mankind" (Q.S.III.90). Here in the Christian story the Holy City—The New Jerusalem is founded

> ...for the healing of the nations
> ...God shall wipe away all tears from their eyes
> ...all proceeding from the throne of the lamb.
> (Revelation 21, 22)

But greater akedic agony awaits humanity before this idyllic and eschatological reconciliation. The tragic tale of the trifurcation continues after the mutual estrangement of the early Muslim centuries. Jews and

Christians are isolated and concentrated within *Dar al Islam*. Despite a glorious and mutually edifying 9th and 10th century when Muslim physicians (Avicenna, Averroes) attend Christian courts and when Muslim scholars translate and preserve Greek science and philosophy, Jewish ghettos and pogroms are incited and all too soon come the crusaders and the inquisition. This terrible breach will fracture the trilateral relation. Judaism is persecuted within Christendom and nearly exterminated in that Shoah. Islam enters a centuries-long degradation under the Ottomans and is finally disgraced as the Christian West dismembers and renames the world in the settlement of the First and Second world wars. Christianity will rise as we shall see as a great world power, though dark clouds hover over the horizon. Let us trace in detail the early medieval trifurcation.

The Crusades

The Seljuk Turks from the Western Orient seized power in Baghdad in 1055 and the Abbasid Caliph recognized them as the military arm of the *Dar-al-Islam*. At this time that expansive realm spanned from the Atlantic Ocean on the African side across to Kabul, even India, with some realms on the North Mediterranean in Europe. Cordova in Spain, Isfahan in Persia and Cairo in Fatima were brilliant cultures of renaissance Islam. The regional autonomy would become a crisis when in 1099, the First Crusade moved across *Dar al-Islam* and attacked Jerusalem.

The Crusaders brutally massacred the Muslim inhabitants of Anatolia at the midway of the Crusade as they had the Jews of the Rhineland at the outset of the Crusade. Establishing Christian (Papal) States, the fragmented Caliphates could offer only token resistance. It was 100 years before the resurgent amirs were able to drive the crusaders from Armenia and Jerusalem. The import of the period is profound, according to Karen Armstrong.

> ...Muslim historians would become preoccupied by the medieval Crusades, looking back with nostalgia to the victorious Saladin (Palestine) and longing for a leader who would be able to contain the neo-crusade of Western imperialism (*Islam*, New York: Modern Library, 2000, p. 95).

In this spirit Michael Doran writing in *Foreign Affairs* ("Somebody Else's Civil War", Jan/Feb 2002, p. 244ff) argues that Osama bin Laden's attacks on the WTS were more intended to unite Global Islam in Armstrong's terms into as a new caliphate than to harm America. If this is the heart of the crisis we call the "War on Terrorism" from New Jersey to the Philippines—through Palestine and Afghanistan—then our response should be to combat radical Islam with a more profound, generous and just

Judaism, Christianity and Islam. If Abrahamic faith is the champion of God-centered faith and the humanely just and compassionate way of life, then the three faiths: Israel, Christendom and moderate Islam should begin to champion the needs of the poor, the refuges, the dispossessed of the world. Just as Islam arises in the world because of the apostasy, idolatry and immorality of Christians and Jews, in akedic resurrection justice-grounding-peace can again call back the presence of God and break the bonds of war.

Such intellectual, cultural and moral unanimity existed for at least a Camelot moment in early medieval Spain. In the Umayyad caliphate of Cordova, Jews, Christians and Muslims lived in total concord and mutual edification. The ethos which fashioned an Averroes (Ibn Rushd 1126-98) needs to be resumed today. Averroes believed that God made the universe for humans to work out its science and justice. The close consultation on faith matters and collaboration in the "good works" of society leads one to believe that this was the "God-intended" mutual enrichment. Societal justice and concord were providentially given in these valences of the Abrahamic heritage. Theologically and biblically speaking peace breaks out when justice undergirds.

Yet, as early as the Berber invasion of Spain this creative unity was disrupted. Jews were now persecuted and Muslims were driven out. Though Jews and Muslims could abide in each other's presence—Israel confident in its *Tanakh* and Talmud and Islam with its Quran and emerging Hadith—Christians had deeper conflict with Judaism. Her enduring presence in the world presented a problem with a philosophy of history centered in the "cross of Christ." The church envisioned herself as the "true Israel" and Israel rejected its "Gentile Mission" leading to a survival-rooted "ghetto-ethnocentricity." A profound distortion had been injected into each faithful body through long centuries of mutual suspicion, hostility and attempted extermination.

At the same time Christianity, as opposed to Islam, knew that it could not exist severed from Judaism. The same scripture animated both faith bodies and a haunting sense of some intertwining destiny pervaded its theology since the Apostle Paul. The same bodily home and Holy Land endured. Even today Jerusalem, Nazareth and Bethlehem provoke holy passion and holy terror in the hearts of Jews and Christians. Though Christian identity is less tied to people and place than to Judaism it does not become a disembodied, ethereal faith. It is grounded in creation and incarnation. Even today theologians like Stanley Hauerwas, Peter Ochs, David Novak, John Levenson and myself search for understandings of the "body" and "land" at least to mute animosity, if not reestablish peace after Shoah. For Christians and Jews, the enigma of Zion sways the future.

For Jews, Messiah, New Testament and the Mass remain problems, to say nothing of the perplexing doctrine of the Trinity. Christians have trouble with Torah, with the body of Israel and with ethnocentricity. To fathom these antinomies remains a theological task for Jews and Christians—a task preliminarily to any future trilogue with Islam. Part of the enduring crisis seems to be the Judeo-centrism of Israel, the Euro-centrism of Christianity and the Arab-centrism of Islam. In dramatic ways the latter two communities have become global and universal in the modern world. The multicultural and interreligious mixing of faiths in modern nations is a sign of hope. Vast communities of Latinos, Africans and Asians constitute contemporary Christianity. Islam has made deep inroads in Africa, Asia, even Europe.

In the Crusades and the concomitant cultural religion, new Christian triumphalism helped sever the ancient sibling faith communities. On the glorious facade of the 13th century cathedrals of St. Denis, Paris, Chartres and Strasbourg the Christian apostles and saints are noble, warrior figures—Greek Gods. Judentum is expressed as a wounded, weak, deformed statue (Chartres Cathedral).

Rather than rise in threatened triumphalism and project therefore a depreciation and will a degradation of the earlier faiths, Christianity should have listened for a deeper signal of Holy history and holy passion in Judaism, then Islam. The growth of Islam in the world, like the *Völkerwanderung* of the Germanic tribes, was the last Semitic migration. This was the portrayal of oriental light to occidental peoples. In terms of my thesis, the inner meaning of Islam, submerged in the present morass of fear and suspicion, is to restore *Taurut* and *injul*, "way" and "gospel," to the world. I have come to see Islam as a prophetic messenger sent by God to the world to restore obedient monotheism to a world dominating Judeo Christian culture, one verging on idolatrous polytheism. Only as Judaism and Christianity withdraw from triumphalist pretensions and Islam rises from besetting humiliation can this deeper vocation be realized. This is the vocation of Torah, *AKEDAH* and Gospel.

When the caliphate passed from Baghdad to Damascus, Islam found its formative and normative center in latent Jewish Christianity, in the Pauline revolution and ultimately in that Judaism cleansed to faith and goodness (justice) by the exile. Now, after the *Reconquista* in Europe, the epicenter of Islam would shift East to the Safavid empire having incorporated many elements of Mongol culture. Islam had broken the bonds of its Arab captivity.

Islam ultimately offsets the occidenttropism of Judaism and Christianity by back-filling the Eastern Asiatic void with a Nestorianism and Monophysitism and taking the great Semitic witness into the orient. Arend van Leewen writes:

The aspect of Islamic expansion which is of greatest moment...for the course of world history is that it succeeded in winning itself a permanent foothold in Asia (*Christianity in World History*, New York: Scribners, 1962, p. 256).

Through Mongols, Indian and Asiatic peoples the faiths of Buddha, the Vedas, Lao Tzu, Kung Fu Tsu (Confucius) and Shinto were confronted with the torah/*AKEDAH* witness, which formed impressive resonance. As India, the Islamic peoples of the southern edge of Russia, China, Korea, Japan, Vietnam, Singapore, Indonesia and the Philippines extend their serene just and communal wisdom into the global *oikumene* in the twenty-first century, hope is felt for the culminating peace and justice of Israel's "light to the Gentiles," Psalm 49.

8
Today: War in Iraq, Palestine, Bosnia, Kosovo, Somalia, and Chechnya

Myriad skirmishes expressed as hundreds of wars—civil, terrorist, religious—have enveloped the world for the last decade. Indeed, The Carter Center, finds the 1990's the most prolific war period in history. These conflicts all represent, in my view, a shaking out of the theological history which this book has sought to comprehend. Orthodox Christendom, the legacy of Constantinian Byzantium—Russia, Greece, Serbia, Croatia—struggles against residual Western Islam in Chechnya, Bosnia and Kosovo. Interestingly, though ignored by anti-American Islamists, America has largely sided with the Muslim peoples in these conflicts, against Christians. The trial in the World War Crimes court in the Hague against the atrocities of ex-Serb president Slobodan Milosevic, witness to the quest for Hebraic justice and peace even against Christian interests. Elsewhere in the world in Palestine, Kenya and Somalia, in the Philippines, Indonesia and Afghanistan, wars continue to erupt.

The immediate global crisis preceding September 11 and the preceding al Qaeda terrorist events in East Africa and Yemen were a series of humanitarian interventions—confrontations with genocidal challenges and war crimes in places like Rwanda, Bosnia, Kosovo and Somalia. The common denominator of these crises was the sending in of armies—perhaps accompanied by NGO's—to offer peacekeeping, suppress clan violence, prevent ethnic-religious genocide and deliver aid. After the devastating bombing, further pulverizing the already exhausted infrastructure of Afghanistan, after the Taliban and al Qaeda, after Osama bin Laden and Mullah Omar have been rooted out, this new kind of fight will be the long-range challenge in Afghanistan, Pakistan and Palestine. We must try to revive the hope that Judaism, Christianity and Islam—Israel, the US and Arabia—can again serve justice and peace around the world.

Somalia

Today, the so-called terrorists and the world anti-terrorist coalition projects its next theatres of engagement as Iraq, Palestine, the Philippines, Georgia, Uzbekistan and Somalia—are mentioned. A brief case study on Somalia and Bosnia will help apply our thesis to the present horizon of global conflict.

> Ye shall have a song as in the night when a holy solemnity is kept... and gladness of heart... (Isaiah 30:29)

Bordered by the Indian Ocean on the East, the Gulf of Aden and the delta of the Red Sea on the North and Ethiopia and Kenya on the West and South, Somalia juts out as a rhino's horn, the protrusion of east Central Africa that before the plate tectonic shift fit simply into the Southern edge of Arabia, now Yemen. Ruled colonially by Italy and Great Britain, Somalia received its independence in 1960. The exuberance of independence was quickly dampened by the cold war in which both Russia and the West exploited the beauteous, wise and poetic ancient land for geopolitical purpose. Its population of some eight million has probably been decimated two or three times by famine and fratricide. In recent years we have witnessed the massive starvation of the population under five years of age making it questionable whether a viable new generation will arise to inherit this good earth.

Constituted by two ethnic communities, the Sab have engaged in sedentary agriculture and the Somali in nomadic herding. The classic Cain and Abel, farmer and herdsman, conflict ensues—clans vying for the father's blessing and the filial legacy. In the brutal infighting that followed the deportation of General Siad Barre in 1989, both fields and flocks were left destitute. Centuries of tribal conflict have been exacerbated by disruption caused by colonialism and cold war. The Italian protectorate, which began in 1885, was united with the post-WWI British Trusteeship in the Northwest in 1950. In 1960 Britain granted independence to its 19th Century protectorate and in that same summer it joined with the Italian jurisdiction to form the Independent Somali Republic. As has so often been the case in Africa, freedom has led to turbulence and chaos.

During the colonial period various parties vied for the limited influence that occupation might allow. SYL (the Somalia Youth League), USP (United Somali Party), and SNL (Somali National League) retained some heritage of the traditional tribal authority. After independence a fragile coalition of these parties sought to govern. Weak administrations served throughout the sixties as cold-war gerrymandering mounted.

The history has verged on a tragic precipice with national and natural calamity always at hand. On October 21, 1969, a Supreme Revolutionary

Council seized power after the president was assassinated and the assembly was dissolved. A severe drought in 1975 killed tens of thousands as nature herself added apocalypse to social antagonisms. Who can forget the moving scene on CBS evening news (December 8, 1992) when correspondent Dan Rather visited Baidoa before the marines arrived. In a makeshift hospital he was asked to hold down and comfort a small child who was writhing in pain after the side of his head had been shot off by violent gunmen. "This is apocalypse now!" Rather cried through his tears.

In the late 1970's, aided by Soviet and Cuban forces, Ethiopian rebels defeated Somali forces in Ethiopia and forced as many as two million Somalian-Ethiopian refugees across the border. Guerilla raids across this border continued until a peace agreement was reached in 1988. Beginning in the early 1980's General Barre's government began what can only be described as a savage and quasi-genocidal war against the three major clans: the Isaac, Ogadan and Hawiye clans ostensibly because of their support of three anti-government parties SNM (Somali National Movement), SPM (Somali Patriotic Movement), and USC (United Somali Congress). The Geneva Conventions and all rules of just-war have been violated as the government, as in Iraq, has looted, raped and killed its own people. By late 1988 tens of thousands had been killed and like numbers of refugees had fled to Ethiopia. In 1992 as clan leaders and gunman-riding-technicals were forced to desist their looting of food and medicines from the NGO's (Non-Governmental Agencies) many fled into hiding across the Ethiopian border. In 1993 a UN peacekeeping force and a strong US ranger contingent held the peace. In a frightful attempt to seize war Lord Mohammed Said that year, 19 GI's, numerous Pakistanis and 1000 Somalis were killed.

Through recent years the twin devastations of famine and civil war have already killed half a million persons and humanitarian appeal to the heart not a strategic appeal to the head has convinced the US to reassert its interest in the region. The strategic concern to protect the Saudi oil fields, the Arabian Gulf and access to the Red Sea has diminished, now the concern focuses on the unconscionable man-made famine and mass starvation of the innocent.

Today, warlords still exploit the poor while cells of al Qaeda foment unrest. The Somali-Yemen axis has been a fulcrum of bin Laden violence. As vividly expressed in Ridley Scott's film after the book *Black Hawk Down*, famine continues, warlords with their technicals terrorize and the poor suffer. Who will champion their sustenance and opportunity: Muslim radicals, the UN peacekeepers or some coalition of these heretofore competitors?

Black Hawk Down, the popular Ridley Scott film in early 2002, romanticizes the events of June 5, 1993. In the aftermath of Special Forces work in Afghanistan after September 11, the military prowess of such

"Green Beret" special forces units and helicopter marines is extolled as was the Israeli's surprise rescue of Entebbe, Uganda in 1976. In actuality, the American attempt to mediate peace was very controversial. With 19 Americans and 1000 Somalis dead, Clinton hightailed it out of there. The engagement became extraction. When several of the American dead were dragged and paraded through the streets before world television, many Americans commented "Why this—for black Africans?" For Keith Richburg, Africa correspondent for the Washington Post, Mogadishu, capital city of Somalia, was close to jungle violence, what he imagined Hobbes' primal state of senseless and persistent aggression to be. Mohammed Aideed, the warlord master, controlling half of Mogadishu, was not only, as the film suggests, a fomenter of continued strife to consolidate and extend his power, he was a 'violent' (Saddam Hussein) toward his own people. He expediently co-opted Islamic ritual where it helped him, neglecting it when it called for justice and peace and care for the hungry and hurting. Nearly one-half million persons had perished from the famine which affected four of Somalia's six million population. Now the clan war would kick the starving masses in their swollen bellies by expropriating their few morsels of food (*Out of America*, New York Books, 1997).

> "These are Sunni Muslims," said one marine, "not the bad Shiiah like in Iran." "Mohammed Farah Aideed," writes Richburg, "seemed crazy, neurotic, evil." While a few yards away people were dropping dead of starvation he sat on cushions and twirled his walking stick." He was a ruthless man who cared little about human life and suffering. One day he embraced Islam beginning his Press Conferences with a prayer to Allah...the next day he was calculating his next bloody ambush (74).

But Aideed was never captured. He disappeared into the country side. After his retreat an uneasy truce eventually settled in. Still in 2002 the unrest and injustice festers discontent and violence. While September 11's terrorists were neighboring Saudis and Egyptians they could just have easily have been Somalis. Today a covert U.S. operation "Mallet" in Kenya prepares to root out insurgent caves in Somalia.

Yet in 1993, the UN and before its abrupt exit, the US, were there as soldiers of righteousness. For was not that Decalogic charter what we were to fight for in life. It was expressed by Isaiah then Jesus:

...to feed the hungry,
...clothe the naked,
...uplift the poor (Isaiah 61:1-2, Luke 4:18,19)

But when we tried that "they shot us in the back…, so we're out-a-here."

In Francis Ford Coppola's *Apocalypse Now*, Martin Sheen plays a lone "tough assignment," anti-terrorist soldier who cries

> …I wanted a mission. And for my sins, they gave me one—brought it to me just like room service. It was a real choice mission (to go after the wily ensconced general played by Marlon Brando). And when it was over, I wouldn't ever want another.

One tension in the akedic/decalogic theology which grounds righteous conflict came out clear in Somalia. On the one hand the Abrahamic convention has people ready to take hold, have hope, move out, resist injustice, whatever the cost. On the other hand it counsels trust and a quiescence to fate. *"Inshallah"* they plead—Allah wills! When Islam, the most fatalistic, destinarian strain of Semitic, Abrahamic faith takes hold among the poor, this acceptance of tragedy, evil, suffering, even injustice, is an ever-present danger. The world must be aware that when Abrahamic (*akedic*-decalogic) righteousness comes to the world it provokes violent persecution from the real "axis of evil" (not that of President Bush).

The question now is: Shall the world, in Abrahamic venture, move out from the old gods of stasis and inaction with the God "on the move,' who Abraham first met "I will be whom I will be" (Exodus 3:14)? Shall warriors in our future confront hunger, violation of human rights, poverty—the ethical yield of living in "the Shemah and Name?" Or shall the world, especially the affluent West, retreat into a military mode of circling the wagons, protecting our privilege, fighting against anyone who would take our stuff from us, or God forbid, even worse, challenge us when we demand our take from the rest of the world? This is the enduring question of Somalia.

Bosnia

At the same time—1994-1995—the free world was also called to the aid of a Muslim people in Bosnia, old Yugoslavia. At the invitation of the great reformed Synagogue in Glen Coe, Illinois I was invited by Rabbi Herb Bronstein to address the congregation. Here is my address:

Dateline: Easter Sunday, 1994
The United States will not defend Gorazde, Bosnia, said Defense Chief William Perry. Falling down to be rolled over as opposing lineman once did to that other William Perry called the Fridge, the US decided not to intervene in Gorazde even in the face of impending ethnic cleansing, rape and genocide. The timing was impeccably ironic—*Yom Hol Shoah*, the Resurrection of the Lord and Passover; High Holy days when those

sublimely gifted—those called out by "the name"—those delivered from oppression and death in the epochal events of Exodus and Easter—those people liberated and ethnically commissioned to *Tikkun Olam*, to serve the world in justice—those committed to see that no people ever again would be harmed, oppressed, raped or herded into gas chambers, liquidated. Yet, these very peacemaking and peacekeeping peoples—those graced by the peculiar love and hope of God—gave up and let Pharaoh, Pilate and Himmel have the day.

Elements of barbaric religious war, Herem, ethnic cleansing, holocaust, holy war and genocide now threaten the globe: Bosnia and Armenia, Ireland, Somalia and Zululand, Sudan and Tajikistan, Afghanistan and Algeria, Palestine, Rwanda and Korea. At the same time the structures of peace-making; NATO and the US; the UN and the Organization of African States; Japan, China and the Asian Confederacy, Israel and her Arab neighbors, have never before been so formidable and so ready to make peace, not war—to beat "swords into plowshares"—to go toward Isaiah's holy mountain, the summit, where nations shall stream for consummate justice. Perhaps we are at an axis point in history, this is a *Kairos* moment, a prophetic breach when God's political history creates crisis and creative possibility. A moment of *Mishpat* and *Zadek*, of judgement and righteousness. Biblical theologies of history hold that high-energy evil often precedes an eruption of peace.

O yes there was and is equivocation to this very hour. General Rose says that NATO may consider offering threat and protection. UN and U.S. authority has drawn the line in ultimatum as it did at Sarajevo. Come Sunday, if the siege on Sarajevo has not stopped, bombing may begin. True to form, the Serbs will probably back off for a few weeks. Generally speaking, however, the world's mood is one of resignation. The problem seems overwhelming and world wide. The malaise of Somalia lingers.

But America and the world are so ill-prepared for peace and justice. In his new book on the current geopolitical crisis *Out of Control: Global Turmoil on the Eve of the Twenty First Century*, Zbignew Brzezinski claims that the UN now enjoys "enlarged authority but ineffective power." Witness the killing of the Pakistani Unit in Somalia or General Rose's contingent in Bosnia. The US has power but no moral authority. The county of Cook whose midland city, our home, is a fire zone, where thirteen are killed in one weekend, has little credibility telling China to get serious on human rights. Perhaps the Harvard University students are right. Genocide maybe happening before our very eyes. Perhaps the most endangered species today is the African-American male. We can spend $30,000 a year to send a young black man to Harvard, or to send him to jail—take your pick. Today, we thrill to see the few survivors—those not dead or in jail marching for Operation Push and the religious coalition at the Robert Taylor homes and Cabrini Green.

Dateline: the Second Sunday of Easter, 1994.

The weekend of Yom Shoah. It is the weekend of marches in Chicago and around the country protesting the massacre at Hebron. Dr. Goldstein had mowed down thirty worshipping Muslims at prayer. American bombers under the flag of NATO scream from a base in Aviano, Italy and attack an Serb artillery command post on the Eastern edge of Gorazde. Then silence...as world leaders concede that Gorazde is at the mercy of the Serbs.

Still, Abraham's vocation calls us on. A liberating and treacherous impulse has been let loose in the world. It springs from a chain of events beginning with the birth and travail of Judaism in world history. It continues with the founding of its revolutionary sect, Christianity. Then it is linked to the sequence of revolutions of freedom, equality, democracy and free enterprise. This provocative impetus and stimulus in world history, especially freedom dissociated from justice, underlies the crisis we face today in Rwanda, Gorazde, South Africa and Washington, DC. If it weren't for the force of human sin distorting the legacy of biblical faith the sequence should read: Judaism, Christianity, Islam, freedom, democracy, solidarity, peace. Now Gorazde, Hebron and Auschwitz punctuate the line of glory.

Dateline: April 15, 1994: The MacNeil-Lehrer News Hour.

Being interviewed is the Vice President of Bosnia, Mr. Elias Janic. He speaks of the immanent humanitarian calamity in Gorazde. "This is Auschwitz—this is genocide," he says. This is a turning point in world history. "The UN is supervising the genocide in Bosnia. I asked for the moralism which is in the American character; the ethical decision (to save or let die) will be made in Washington, London and Paris."

To further explore the thesis that I have offered that the historical residue of Judaism must be ethically reoriented away from enterprise and aggression to justice and peace, let me offer some reflections on history as a source of ethics, on the radical subversion that genocide represents. Then finally we return full circle to what the historical ethics of justice and peace receive in all the Bosnias of contemporary history!

First some notes about history and ethics. Like nature or the will of God, history is a source of ethics. History is a selected fund of those events and interpretation of events by which we seek to give meaning to what has gone before. History, thus, is value laden.

Search the past, the time before you were born, all the way back to the time when God created man on the earth. Search the entire earth. Has anything as great as this ever happened before? Has anyone ever heard of anything like this? Have any people ever lived after hearing a god speak to them from a fire, as you have? Has any god ever dared to go and take a people from another nation and make them his own, as the Lord your God did for you in Egypt? Before your very eyes he used his great power and strength; he brought plagues and war, worked miracles and wonders, and caused terrifying things to happen. The Lord has shown you this, to prove to you that he alone is God and that there is no other. He let you hear his voice from heaven so that he could instruct you; and here on earth he let you see his holy fire, and he spoke to you from it. Because he loved your ancestors, he chose you, and by his great power he himself brought you out of Egypt (Deuteronomy 4: 32-37).

Indeed, for history to be morally instructive we have to draw lessons. Recall the oft-quoted wisdom of Santayana that those who ignore history are doomed to repeat it. One wonders today as conflict bogs down in the Middle East or Eastern Europe whether the exact opposite of the supposed "lesson" of the Cold War history of nuclear deterrence is in fact true. In that view the only prevention to war was the perpetual fear of the nuclear weapons we continued to stockpile. Could we not as easily argue on historical grounds that since Hiroshima and the surrender of the Japanese in 1945 that no war has ever been won or concluded without nuclear weapons. Unless you take seriously skirmishes like the Falklands, Grenada, and Panama, all other post-Hiroshima wars have been indecisive and finally unresolved—Korea, Viet Nam, Iran/Iraq, the African and Central American conflicts, The Gulf War and Yugoslavia, Somalia and Afghanistan.

When we contemplate the contemporary genocides or the archetypal Holocaust of the European Jews, we face one of the deepest mysteries in history. As Arno Mayer of Princeton University has shown, history's greatest enigma is fundamentally a question of theology. Judeocide across the millennia and the decade of the crucifixion of Jesus hover in the dark background when we ponder the genocide of six million Jews in Europe in the 1930's and 1940's. Entitling his book from a text of Solomon bar Simpson in 1096, Mayer quotes:

No one was found to stand in the breach.
Why did the heavens not darken
And the stars not withhold their radiance.
Why did not the sun and the moon turn dark.

The word genocide (*gens*: a race, tribe; *cide*: killing) was coined by jurist Raphael Lemkin as he sought to develop support for the United Nations "Genocide" convention passed in 1948. By definition genocide is "a coordinated plan of different actions aiming at the destruction of essential foundations of the life of national groups, with the aim of annihilating the groups themselves." Beyond the prototype genocides of the Armenians in the second decade and of the European Jews in the fourth and fifth decades of this century, Leo Kuper groups a series of modern political and genocidal events as fulfilling this definition. These include: the Russian-contrived famine of the Ukraine (1932), the US and British bombing of Hiroshima, Nagasaki, Dresden and Hamburg; the massacres by the communists in Indonesia (1965) of the noncommunists in Kampuchea (1975), the Tibetans by China (1950), and the Bangladeshi by the Bengali (1971).

The European Holocaust has taken such universal significance because it happened in the heart of Judeo-Christian civilization, that very civilization which had brought universal history to the world, but out of the Greek and Roman *Oikumene*. Christian civilization—the now waning, arrogant and secularized vestige of the Holy Roman Empire, *Corpus Christianum Res Publica*, unleashed the sin of the world, the new crucifixion of the Holy One of God. In a grotesque act of rational, technical, medical, political. Ecclesial, cultural, and historical evil all humanity wandered astray and we lost our way in the world.

Our only hope now is to shun all pretense and in a great act of repentance and renewal of life before the God of Israel and of the Universe, examine afresh who we are, recover God's inaugurating, sustaining, and finishing purposes in history and in nature and reclaim our origination, constitution, and destination as a human family on planet earth. Then with a covenant of faith reestablished, as Israel was reestablished in the Deuteronomic reform, we can reestablish those derived covenants of life with life and offer protection and edification in the creation. If we fail, all that awaits us is to perish with the whole world in some final holocaust where the abomination will be the odor and smoke of nuclear, chemical, and biological destruction—and a bang, and a whimper.

How does history, even genocidal history (remember Moses' rising in Egypt begins with infanticide [also the] Passover and Herod's infanticide at the time of Jesus' birth) viewed in light of Exodus, crucifixion, and holocaust, influence morality? The impact is clear regarding human death. The ameliorative reach of God into our suffering and death grounds imperatives to save and to not kill. The primal NO against killing and YES for protecting life has resounded through human conscience since Cain and Abel and is directed against all forms of fratricide, genocide, infanticide, and suicide. Killing is to seek to expel God from the cosmos and therefore obliterate the human soul within us. In a day of prayer for peace convened by Pope John Paul II at Assisi, Italy, a Jain priest prayed fervently:

> Whom thou intendest to kill is, in truth
> None other then thyself...
> Violence, in fact, is the knot of bondage
> It, in fact, is delusion
> It, in fact, is death
> It, in fact, is hell.

Can we ever say with Cicero, who upon hearing of the murder of Caesar, exclaimed "O noble deed!'"? Can we condone the conspiracy of Dietrich Bonhoeffer, Hans von Dohnanyi, and others who in the July 20 movement sought to assassinate Adolph Hitler? Will the air force officers slain in the attempt on Saddam Hussein's life ever be heroes? The story is eventually told and full narrative reveals character. "History never repeats itself," said Voltaire, "man always does." Fallen human beings kill when they should not, and do not when they should. This might be the primary moral lesson in history. In holy genocide, Henry VIII ordered his commander to "sack Leith and burn and subvert it, putting man, woman and child to fire and sword without exception."

> Israel did it with the Amalekites;
> Hitler did it with Israel;
> Turkey with Armenia;
> Serbia with Bosnia;
> Hutu with Tutsi;
> and on and on...

unless we hear again the prophetic word: "I set before you good and evil, life and death...CHOOSE LIFE." (This section is drawn from my book *Birth Ethics*, p. 108 ff).

Where does history as ethics and genocide as antihistory leave us? I can only offer a modest proposal. In the Isaianic vision, nations one day will come up to the holy summit (Jerusalem) for arbitration and reconciliation. Here we will beat swords into plowshares and learn war no more. Here shalom and the knowledge of YAHWEH will fill the earth as the waters cover the sea (Isaiah 11:9). Can the United Nations or the penultimate subsidiaries—NATO, the Organization of African or Latin American States, the Asian Confederation—can these political and geopolitical entities embody this eschatological vision of justice-grounded peace? Surely it can, for there is nothing else but a perpetual acceleration of horror where the powerful devour the weak.

The time has come in history when the moral charter offered the world in the Abrahamic peoples is the only vision that can save the human race and the planet. We need to get off the misguided path which is the bible's notion of sin. On this path we proceed from liberation to freedom, to enterprise, to consumption, to inequality, to calamity. The path to which the prophets call is liberation, freedom, equalizing-democracy, social and economic justice in the world, reconciliation, and peace. When hatred rules the world redemption will not come.

> Let the day be near when love will rule this world.
> Pray God place into our outstretched yearning hands the power of peace.

Conclusion
The war on terrorism stands in a long history of warfare (from the Holy War of ancient Israel through Constantine's war to establish a Christian empire, through the crusades, Cousins' Wars, to the century's wars for freedom against the tyrannies of fascism, communism and to myriad "humanitarian wars." Religion's history (The rise of Judaism, Christianity, and Islam) gives us guidance in its central normative paradigm TORAH-AKEDAH-that sacrifice will lead to freedom, redeeming the world as justice grounds authentic peace. This is the "life-way" worth defending and extending—worth fighting for.)

This brief study is dedicated to you, my readers, as you join that Holy War, that Crusade, that Jihad.

Kenneth L. Vaux
Evanston, Illinois
May 2002